The Confident Speaker's Handbook

A Practical, Hands-on Approach to Public Speaking

Fourth Edition

Thomas Valasek

Raritan Valley Community College

Kendall Hunt
publishing company

www.kendallhunt.com
Send all inquiries to:
4050 Westmark Drive
Dubuque, IA 52004-1840

CONTENTS

P R E F A C E

One of the advantages of using *The Confident Speaker's Handbook* with students in my speech classes at Raritan Valley Community College is that they can provide direct and immediate feedback about what works and what doesn't work in this book. And their feedback has been consistently positive. Most students find the *Speaker's Handbook* relevant, helpful, and accessible. The stalwart chapters, not surprisingly, are those on managing anxiety about public speaking, developing basic presentation skills, and developing introductions and conclusions. Consequently, I fine-tuned these chapters in this edition but left them essentially intact. Other chapters, such as those on preparing and using visual aids and on handling a question-and-answer session, I have revised, expanded, or updated more extensively. There are also new examples of student speeches and visual aids for critiquing, and a new chapter on preparing and delivering team presentations, which several of my faculty colleagues requested.

I am grateful to my colleagues in the Communication and Languages Department at Raritan Valley Community College for their many thoughtful comments and suggestions for this new edition, and especially to David Sandler who sagely recommended a more workable order for the chapters and offered supplemental material for the chapter on Q&A.

Thomas Valasek
Raritan Valley Community College

Public Speaking: A Life Skill and a Skill for Life

"Speaking skills help us live more fully and freely, knowing we can share our thoughts and passions in a public forum without feeling overwhelmed by fear and anriety."

Very few of us are born dynamic, confident public speakers. Most people have to work hard to become an effective speaker, even those with natural talent. *The Confident Speaker's Handbook* is designed to help you become a better public speaker as expeditiously as possible. As the title indicates, this book is "a practical, hands-on approach to public speaking." The book's methodology is based on the belief that public speaking is an activity, partly intellectual and partly physical, that you can learn and eventually master by practicing a few important fundamentals. *The Confident Speaker's Handbook* presents these fundamentals simply and directly, and tries to help you apply them quickly and effectively. As you read the text, hopefully you will see that it is indeed meant to be a handbook, a handy reference that you can pick up any time—today or ten years from today—when you have a question or problem about a speech you're giving. In every chapter you will find practical suggestions for improving both the content and delivery of speeches. Practical tips are included for every important aspect of public speaking, from "how to manage anxiety about public speaking" to "how to handle a question-and-answer session."

Drawing on decades of personal experience teaching, coaching, and practicing public speaking, *The Confident Speaker's Handbook* focuses heavily on aspects of public speaking that are especially important for beginning speakers, such as managing anxiety about public speaking, developing effective introductions and conclusions, preparing and using visual aids, and rehearsing speeches efficiently. There are chapters specifically devoted to these concerns, and they are also reinforced throughout the handbook. This book focuses most on what works best, both for novices and for old pros, to build confident public speakers.

The chapters in this book begin with a brief "scenario" based on experiences of real people, either from the academic or the business world, who learned to overcome their fears and solve problems about public speaking. These real-life examples, hopefully will serve as models and as inspiration for you. Remember, these speakers struggled with the same difficulties and insecurities about public speaking that you may feel right now. They all learned how to overcome them and present successful speeches. With enough commitment and effort, so will you.

Although she already had a bachelor's degree, Donna enrolled at Raritan Valley Community College for career retraining after she was squeezed out of a job because of corporate downsizing. Donna requested a waiver from a communication course, "Presentation Skills for Business and Professions," which was required in the multimedia communication program she was pursuing. Donna argued that she already had these skills; she had made many presentations in the corporate world and had been responsible for most of the major presentations in her division. She thought the course would be much too basic for her. In fact, Presentation Skills is a hands-on, media-intensive presentation course, and the skills it covers are not necessarily the same ones she learned in the field. Donna was finally persuaded to take the course because we promised that if she invested in it she would improve significantly as a presenter and carry her already proficient public speaking skills to a higher level.

Some time after Donna finished the multimedia program, she sent a note mentioning that she was employed again, using her skills in a new communication field. She said that the courses she took prepared her well for this new job, particularly Presentation Skills, which helped her showcase her talents, both in other college courses and ultimately in the workplace. Finally, she wrote about how the course affected her personally:

> *You are the only teachers I ever met who* guaranteed *I'd be better*
> *coming out of a course. I thought you were either nuts or just full of*
> *yourselves, but you were right. I am so much more aware of myself and*
> *my skills as a speaker now, not only in formal but also in informal*
> *situations. I'm better in interviews, better in groups, and more confident*
> *in general. I've just joined the speaker's bureau at my public library. I*
> *think I was always good at presenting, but now I really enjoy it.*

In closing, Donna offered to come back and speak to current classes about the importance of presentation skills.

Naturally, speech teachers and coaches are always pleased to receive testimonials from former students like Donna about the value of good public speaking skills for their professional careers and their lives. But we do not need testimonials to feel secure about the importance of these skills. Donna's note only reinforces our experience that if you are willing to invest some time and energy into building presentation skills, the payback over a lifetime can be enormous. What students like Donna have come to appreciate is that public speaking is a skill for life, a skill that can be an asset in your academic and professional career as well as in your personal life. The ability to present your ideas articulately and confidently is "money in the bank" that you may draw upon many times throughout your life.

Understandably, many of you reading this book right now are taking a public speaking or presentation skills course because it is required in your academic program, not because you really want to. You are probably feeling nervous and insecure about speaking in front of a group of people you don't know. If you could find a way to get out of it, you would jump at it. It is a well-known fact that fear of public speaking is one of strongest and most common anxieties people have today. But it is a less well-known fact that, for many people, public speaking is an exhilarating experience and a wonderful confidence builder.

We offer you the same guarantee Donna received: No matter where your public speaking skills are right now, if you make a commitment, invest some of yourself, and practice the basic principles and guidelines outlined in this handbook, you *will* become a more competent and confident public speaker. You will gain a skill that will serve you well in the classroom, in the workplace, and in your personal life.

A SKILL FOR THE CLASSROOM

As Donna observed in her note, developing skills to deliver organized, well-structured class presentations can be valuable in other college courses. Students often report that even before they finish a speech class, they feel more confident about class presentations. They are more willing to choose an oral report in courses where that is an option, knowing they have more confidence in their presentation skills. Further along in their academic careers students like Donna can sometimes "ace" a senior seminar or a graduate course because dynamic class presentations help them showcase their research or special area of expertise. Knowing that you have basic presentation skills under your belt may also help you feel more confident about participating in class or small-group discussions.

A SKILL FOR THE WORKPLACE

Each year the National Association of Colleges and Employers (NACE) surveys about 3,000 employers nationwide about their hiring plans for new college graduates. One of the questions the NACE Job Outlook survey asks employers is to rank how important certain qualities are when they consider hiring a new employee.

In the figure on the next page you can see that in the NACE Job Outlook 2012 report, employers ranked "Ability to verbally communicate with persons inside and outside the organization," with a rating of 4.59 (out of a possible 5.00), near the top of the list of skills and qualities they are looking for in new employees. This falls right behind "Ability to work in a team structure," with a rating of 4.60. The survey clearly shows that employers consider communication skills for new employees more important than the ability to make decisions and solve problems or to obtain and process information, and considerably more important than proficiency with computer software programs or the ability to sell or influence others. Ironically, the NACE survey also shows that verbal communication skills are near the top of the list of skills that employers find most lacking in college graduates. Some employers even comment that students' poor presentation skills become evident in job interviews.

The next time you visit a career fair on your campus or talk with a corporate recruiter, ask what employers are looking for in their "new hires." You will find that communication skills are at or near the top of everyone's list. And the communication skill that is in greatest demand in today's high-tech business world is the ability to communicate effectively to a group. Peggy Noonan, speechwriter for former presidents Ronald Reagan and George H. W. Bush, says in her book *Simply Speaking:*

> *As more and more businesses become involved in the new media technologies, as we become a nation of fewer widgets and more Web sites, a new premium has been put on the oldest form of communication: the ability to stand and say what you think in front of others.*

In her note Donna indicated how confident and comfortable she feels in interviews, in groups, and on the job as a result of her experience in the presentation skills course. She didn't mention (until later) that she got her new job partly because her portfolio includes a PowerPoint presentation on "The Use of Color in Advertising," which she created and presented in the class she wanted to waive. In this instance, we can trace a direct connection between a specific class project and a job opportunity. However, the word in the workplace these days is that your technical or professional skills get you hired, but your communication skills get you noticed and promoted.

A SKILL FOR LIFE

Many students finish a public speaking course with a great sigh of relief and say to themselves: "That's behind me. I'm never going to stand up to speak in front of a group again. I'm going to be a veterinarian, or a funeral director." But these students are wrong.

Skill/Quality	Weighted average rating*
Ability to work in a team structure	4.60
Ability to verbally communicate with persons inside and outside the organization	4.59
Ability to make decisions and solve problems	4.49
Ability to obtain and process information	4.46
Ability to plan, organize, and prioritize work	4.45
Ability to analyze quantitative data	4.23
Technical knowledge related to the job	4.23
Proficiency with computer software programs	4.04
Ability to create and/or edit written reports	3.65
Ability to sell or influence others	3.51

*5-point scale, where 1 = Not important; 2 = Not very important; 3 = Somewhat important; 4 = Very important; and 5 = Extremely important

Reprinted from *Job Outlook 2012,* with permission of the National Association of Colleges and Employers, copyright holder.

Throughout our lives we may be members of parent-teacher associations, church or civic groups, charity or social organizations, clubs or teams. And occasionally we may be called upon to "say a few words." You may be asked to address the PTA about an upcoming bake sale, present trophies at the youth soccer banquet, or deliver the eulogy at your grandfather's funeral. Knowing some fundamentals about how to present yourself before an audience will help you meet these speaking occasions with confidence and poise.

When we say that speaking skills are for life, we mean that in very practical ways we can use them all our lives. But in another sense, this statement also means that speaking skills are *for* life, that they allow us to live more fully and freely, knowing that we may welcome opportunities to share our most important thoughts and passions in a public forum without feeling overwhelmed by fear and anxiety of public speaking.

Managing Anxiety about Public Speaking

*"With preparation and practice, you will teach those butterflies
in your stomach how to fly in formation"*

Michael is a successful corporate manager who participated in an intensive three-day Presentation Skills Workshop in Philadelphia. By almost every measure Michael is a superb public speaker. He is pleasant, animated, well-organized, and has a knack for telling witty anecdotes that are right on the money. His presentations had only one failing. The second the speech ended, it was as if someone had turned off a switch in Michael. He immediately lost all the animation and personality in his face, his body sagged, and he left the room abruptly.

Michael was stunned to find out in evaluations from his peers in the workshop that this behavior was perceived as rude and condescending. Somewhat embarrassingly, he confided that speaking in front of the group made him so nervous and tied his stomach up in such a knot that he had to run out quickly at the end of his presentation and throw up. Moreover, Michael was certain that everyone in the audience could see this nervousness in his face and body during the presentation.

When Michael looked closely at a video of his presentation to identify specific signs of nervousness, he was surprised to discover that he did not appear nervous at all. In fact, he had to admit that he looked fairly comfortable and relaxed. With that realization in mind, Michael began developing a strategy to alleviate some of his nervousness. He learned that

ANXIETY MONSTER

▼ **Draw your anxiety monster below:**

Dawn Reilly
RVCC student

2

by interacting with the audience more and by taking pauses to slow his speaking pace, he could relax enough to get through speeches without feeling he had to throw up.

Michael has become a very accomplished public speaker who now admits that he "almost likes getting up in front of an audience" because he enjoys the successful results. He still gets nervous, but now understands how to manage his nervousness and make it work to his advantage. "I still get a knot in my stomach when I have to speak," he says. "But now I know how to slow down and untie it."

Fear of public speaking, known as *communication apprehension* among communication educators, is one of the most common anxieties people experience. Although Michael's reaction may be somewhat extreme, he is certainly not unique in feeling extremely nervous about speaking in front of an audience. This is why many major corporations send their employees to presentation skills workshops for the kind of training Michael received, training that can sometimes be very exclusive and expensive. For example, Dorothy Sarnoff, a former actress and opera singer, and now one of the most sought-after speech consultants in New York City, runs a company called Speech Dynamics Inc. that has helped many of the country's highest-paid corporate executives improve their public speaking skills. Many of the CEOs who come to her for help, paying thousands of dollars for a few sessions of private tutoring, are terrified of giving a speech. Joan Ganz Cooney, for instance, founder of the Children's Television Network, admits that public speaking has been a trauma for her for many years. "I thought it was my dirty little secret," she says. "I get over my nervousness for one speech—and it comes back full force for the next." Some executives admit that they get heart palpitations if they are even asked to introduce themselves at a business meeting. Dorothy Sarnoff says the worst case of communication anxiety she ever encountered was the general counsel of a large corporation who was so shaken before an important speech at the Waldorf-Astoria Hotel in New York City that he faked a heart attack so he wouldn't have to go on.

If you think you are the only person in your speech class or presentation skills workshop who is scared and anxious to stand up and speak in public, you are very mistaken. In fact, you are very normal. In many surveys people consistently cite public speaking as one of the most stressful activities they face, often ranking it as more stressful than root canal surgery or financial bankruptcy. No matter how distinguished or nonchalant they may appear at the podium, most public speakers, even professionals, feel nervous about giving an important speech or business presentation. Television commentator Edwin Newman once said that "the only difference between the professionals and the novices is that the pros have taught the butterflies to fly in formation."

So, if you feel nervous about public speaking, you can take consolation in the fact that you are not alone. And more importantly, you are not alone in being able to manage your nervousness, and perhaps, like Michael, to *use* it to become a successful speaker who "almost likes" public speaking. Many others have learned to manage their butterflies successfully. So can you.

ESTABLISHING REALISTIC EXPECTATIONS

It is helpful if you begin with realistic expectations about public speaking. If you think a speech class or workshop is going to free you forever of communication anxiety, you will probably be disappointed. For many people the anxiety never goes away. There are some highly accomplished speakers, as Michael, Joan Ganz Cooney, and Edwin Newman can testify, who get nervous every time they address an audience. But they are accomplished public speakers because they have learned to manage anxiety and channel nervous energy in constructive ways.

The presentation setting can sometimes affect the anxiety level a speaker feels. For example, a college professor or a corporate trainer probably does not feel nervous about presenting to students or trainees. That's what they do for a living. But ask the professor to deliver the faculty commencement address at graduation or the trainer to present a report to the board of directors, and they will almost certainly experience communication apprehension. Experienced public speakers know that some speaking situations are more stressful than others, and prepare accordingly.

It also helps to remember that a bit of nervousness before a presentation may be useful. Pumping adrenaline into the system is the body's way of responding to stress and helping it function at a higher level. Many great athletes get nervous before an important race or game, sometimes to the extent that they throw up. And musicians, dancers, and actors often feel "performance anxiety" before they go on stage. But to be successful at what they do, they must learn to relax and concentrate on the task at hand and use the extra adrenaline to keep them in the "zone" where they achieve their best results.

Public speaking is a high-energy physical activity, and extra adrenaline can help speakers excel at it. In fact, it may be counterproductive to wish for nervousness to go away entirely. The truth is, if the speech is important, the speaker is bound to feel anxious about it. And being keyed up can help make presentations more energetic and lively. Studies with students experiencing math anxiety, for example, have shown that a moderate level of nervousness helps students concentrate and perform better on exams; but beyond that level nervousness interferes with concentration and decreases test performance. The same principle applies to public speaking. The key to success is to manage anxiety so that it works *for* you, not against you.

So, instead of trying to make the fear of public speaking go away, think about taking advantage of it to sharpen your concentration, focus your attention, and invigorate your presentation style. Remember that there is nothing intrinsically fearful about public speaking. Many people become quite comfortable giving speeches; some even enjoy and look forward to them. Much of the fear people experience about public speaking comes from not knowing what to say, or what to do, when they give a speech. If you take steps to address these two concerns, you will become more confident about public speaking, and conversely less fearful.

ANXIETY MONSTER

▼ **Draw your anxiety monster below:**

James Kroner
RUCC student

The rest of this chapter focuses on strategies for managing anxiety about public speaking. First, are some general strategies you can use while planning and preparing your speech, then some specific strategies you can use while actually delivering your presentation.

STRATEGIES FOR MANAGING COMMUNICATION ANXIETY

Confront Your Fear

The following Anxiety Monster Exercise was developed by Prof. Catherine Blackburn at Brookdale Community College in New Jersey to help students in speech classes manage communication anxiety.

There's a Bugs Bunny cartoon called *Hair-Raising Hare* where Bugs meets a heart-shaped monster who is determined to eat him. Bugs first tries to run away from this monster but then tries to fend him off with some of his usual antics. At one point he chides the monster for having ugly nails, and begins to give him a manicure. He talks continually to the monster, chattering about what interesting lives monsters must lead, distracting him while he prepares to spring his next trick.

We all have a public speaking anxiety monster within us who wants to eat us up. It is very persistent, attacking and eroding our confidence at every opportunity. Like Bugs, our first impulse may be to run away from this monster as fast and as far as possible. We try to fend it off by avoiding public speaking altogether. Eventually, however, the monster catches up with us, and we are forced to deal with it. But if we can face up to the monster, and confront it, we have a better chance of overcoming it.

One way to confront your anxiety monster is to draw a picture of it. Trying to visualize the monster, the setting in which it appears, and the effect it has on you is a good first step toward dealing with your fears about public speaking. At the end of this chapter is a blank worksheet on which you can draw your anxiety monster. You don't need to be an artist to make this exercise work for you. Just sketch freely, trying to capture the scariest features and characteristics of your monster. Once you visualize it, you will have a clearer idea of what kind of monster you are dealing with, and perhaps some clues about how to control it. Throughout this chapter you will see examples of anxiety monsters drawn by students in speech classes at Raritan Valley Community College.

Another way to confront your fear of public speaking is to identify specific indicators of anxiety that emerge when you deliver a presentation. For example, note any physical indicators you experience, such as increased heart rate, flushed face, sweaty palms, or butterflies in the stomach. These indicators, in fact, commonly show up in anxiety monster drawings. There are also psychological indicators, such as self-consciousness, fear of losing one's train of thought, or concerns about being judged by the audience, which are sometimes more difficult to draw.

ANXIETY MONSTER

▼ **Draw your anxiety monster below:**

Evil Confidence and Content eating Monkey

I have nothing import-ant to say

Rebekah Buczynski
RUCC student

Resources are available that can help you identify and assess such communication anxiety indicators. One of the most useful is the Communication Anxiety Inventory (CAI), developed in the mid-1980s, which asks speakers to rate their level of anxiety with specific physical or psychological indicators immediately after delivering a presentation (see Figure 1.1). The CAI lists 20 simple statements, such as, "My heart seemed to beat faster than usual" or "I worried about what others thought of me." If you were using the CAI

Communication Anxiety Inventory

Instructions: The following items describes how people communicate in various situations. Choose the number from the following scale that best describes how you felt during the communication experience you *just completed*.

Not at all	Somewhat	Moderately so	Very much so
1	2	3	4

1. I felt tense and nervous.
2. I felt self-confident while talking.
3. While talking, I was afraid of making an embarrassing or silly slip of the tongue.
4. I worried about what others thought of me.
5. I felt calm when I was talking.
6. I felt ill at ease using gestures when I spoke.
7. I could not think clearly when I spoke.
8. My listener(s) seemed interested in what I had to say.
9. I felt poised and in control while I was talking.
10. My body felt tense and stiff while I was talking.
11. My words became confused and jumbled when I was speaking.
12. I felt relaxed when I was talking.
13. My fingers and hands trembled when I was speaking.
14. I felt I had nothing worthwhile to say.
15. I had a "deadpan" expression on my face when I spoke.
16. I found myself talking faster or slower than usual.
17. While speaking, it was easy to find the right words to express myself.
18. I felt awkward when I was talking.
19. My heart seemed to beat faster than usual.
20. I maintaind eye contact when I wanted to.

Note: Reverse coding on Items 2, 5, 8, 9, 12, 17, and 20 before summing.

FIGURE 1.1

From *Communication Quarterly, Volume 34, No. 2, Spring 1986* by Steven Booth-Butterfield and Malloy Gould. Copyright © 1986 by Routledge. Reprinted by permission of Taylor & Francis Ltd. http://www.tandf.co.uk/journals

survey after a presentation, you would describe your reaction to each statement on a scale of 1 (*Not at all*) to 4 (*Very much so*). The CAI inventory results can help speakers, especially less-experienced speakers, become more aware of the overall level of their communication anxiety as well as how it manifests itself, both physically and psychologically. Therefore, they will have a better idea of what nervous reactions to expect when presenting and, hopefully, how to prepare beforehand to manage them better.

Make Fear Your Ally

Another strategy for dealing with fear of public speaking has been employed by great individuals in many walks of life—soldiers and athletes, prominent political and business figures, ordinary people facing extraordinary circumstances in their lives: Make fear your ally. Use it to find strength and courage in yourself, to reinforce your determination and character. Turn your fear of public speaking into a personal challenge. If you were playing one-on-one basketball, you would try to exude strength and self-confidence because your opponent would have an advantage over you if he sensed weakness or lack of confidence. As a matter of principle and personal pride, never announce your butterflies to the audience, and try to control behaviors that may betray any nervousness. Learn to make those butterflies fly in formation!

Keep in mind that it is the speaker's responsibility to help the audience feel comfortable, and they will not feel at ease if they sense you are anxious or insecure about your presentation. Besides, announcing your nervousness may undermine your credibility, and could even become the primary focus of the audience's attention.

Commit Yourself

Anytime an occasion to speak presents itself, whether voluntary or mandatory, there is a critical moment when the prospective speaker has to make a commitment, to "sign on the dotted line" so to speak. This is a terrifying moment for many people because they feel there is no turning back. But, from another perspective, this moment could also be the beginning of the road to success.

There is, however, another level of commitment even after you sign on the dotted line—the psychological commitment to do the job well. This is like signing a contract with yourself to give the presentation your best effort. By committing yourself psychologically to the speech from the very beginning, you are inviting and encouraging success, and therefore helping yourself overcome one of the biggest reasons for being nervous about speeches—fear of failure. How much success can you rightfully expect with a speech if you don't fully commit yourself to it?

Think Positively

It is easy to find reasons not to make a speech. But try thinking of the potential benefits that will result from your speech. Your presentation may give the audience useful information or an amusing diversion. It may help someone make an important decision, or change someone's life in ways you cannot imagine. As a speaker, it is very gratifying to receive comments like these after a speech:

You made me see school taxes in a totally different light.

You helped me realize how important it is to perform some kind of community service.

You made me appreciate how interesting and enjoyable it can be to read fairy tales as a grown up.

Your presentation may also directly benefit you, immediately in your academic or professional endeavors, or down the road with skills that make your life more interesting and productive. A great presentation might earn you a high grade or a promotion. And if you can't think of any particular benefits, create a reward for yourself, such as concert tickets or a special dinner, for giving the presentation. The more you invest psychologically in your speech, the better your chances will be for success, both with the presentation itself and with managing communication anxiety.

Prepare Thoroughly

It stands to reason that you cannot feel confident and relaxed about a speech if you are not prepared to present it. In fact, there is good reason to feel nervous because you know that the lack of preparation will almost certainly make you look bad. To be an accomplished public speaker you need to prepare not only your material, but also yourself.

The first way to prepare for a speech is to do your homework. Even if you are knowledgeable about your subject, you still need to organize the material for each specific presentation, check that your resources are current and accurate, and select interesting and relevant examples suited to your audience. Doing your homework will also help you prepare for questions or discussion that may follow the presentation. (Chapter 2 talks more about how to research and organize your speech.)

Whenever possible, prepare visual aids for your presentation because they can help you focus and remember your speech, which will therefore make you feel more confident and less anxious. Visual aids provide a handy overview and outline of your speech, both for you and the audience. (Chapter 5 discusses how to prepare and use visual aids effectively.)

But besides preparing your material, you also need to prepare yourself to anticipate problems or distractions that may interfere with your presentation. If you know, for example, that you have a tendency to talk too fast when you are nervous, you should practice speaking extra slowly and using pauses when you rehearse. In this way you will reinforce behaviors that help you deal with anxiety when presentation time arrives. (Chapter 6 discusses strategies for rehearsing your speech.)

Imagine Success

Researchers at Washington State University in Pullman conducted a study to find out whether visualization techniques could reduce the discomfort many people feel when

Justin Payne

ANXIETY MONSTER

▼ **Draw your anxiety monster below:**

Justin Payne
RVCC student

faced with public speaking. They studied 107 speech students who experienced communication anxiety, dividing them into four groups. One group practiced visualization during the week before giving a speech. A control group was given no training at all. The two remaining groups practiced other commonly used confidence-building techniques: one learned muscle relaxation, and the other learned positive thinking. By comparing visualization to other "placebo" techniques, not just to a control group, the researchers were ensuring that any effects they found were actually due to visualization training, not just to extra attention those students received.

Students in the visualization group were coached to imagine themselves in the best possible scenario for the day of the speech, down to the smallest details: dressing exactly right; feeling focused, confident, and thoroughly prepared; delivering an interesting, articulate speech that is well received; enjoying audience reactions to humorous or insightful comments.

The researchers found that students who used visualization had significantly less communication apprehension than students in the control group or in the two other groups.

Visualization is a way of rehearsing a presentation mentally with expectations of positive results. You can use visualization throughout the process of preparing your speech, continually refining the visualized scenario to reinforce mentally the impression you want to make on the audience and the feeling you want to have about presenting the speech. It is important to imagine the speech as a *positive* experience and to incorporate as much detail as possible. The knowledge that visualization works—that imagining success can actually make it happen—can boost your confidence and relieve some of your anxiety about a speech.

Practice Relaxation

Remember that public speaking is partly a physical activity. Perhaps it is not as physically intricate or demanding as square dancing, playing basketball, or performing martial arts, but, like these activities, effective public speaking requires good posture, balance, and body control. And just like a good dancer, athlete, or martial artist, a successful public speaker is able to relax during the presentation and make it look easy and natural.

Telling someone who is nervous about giving a speech to "just relax" is like telling an insomniac to "just go to sleep." It's easy advice to give but difficult to carry out at the time it is needed. However, you can learn to relax by practicing relaxation techniques, both while preparing and while delivering a presentation. You may already have learned ways to relax for sports, arts, or theater; and you can apply these same relaxation techniques to public speaking.

One can practice many forms of relaxation to manage communication anxiety, especially before the speech. Many people find that physical exercise (a brisk walk, jog, or bicycle ride, for example) helps them reduce stress and keep a clear mind. Others try to imagine themselves in a peaceful place (by the ocean or in a quiet forest) where they feel calm and focused. Some people listen to quiet music to relax; others practice meditation. There are different kinds of meditation, but they all involve settling the body into a comfortable position in a quiet setting, clearing the mind of mundane thoughts and concerns, and focusing on one thing—breathing, a mantra, an image, or a peaceful thought—in order to achieve calmness and heightened consciousness.

Commercially available relaxation or stress-reduction tapes are common, both in audio and video formats. Often these tapes are available in college or public libraries or can be easily downloaded. If you find that one of these relaxation techniques helps you reduce stress, use it to manage your anxiety about public speaking. It is especially important to practice relaxation when you prepare and rehearse your speech, anticipating where and how your anxiety monster may show up when you actually present it.

Focus on Communication, Not Performance

An article in *Psychology Today,* entitled "Taking the Terror out of Talk," argues that one of the most effective strategies for managing anxiety about public speaking is "to view speeches as communication rather than performance." This means that speakers should focus on sharing their ideas with the audience rather than on analyzing or criticizing how well they present them. Focusing on communication helps you feel that effective public speaking is more like ordinary conversation than like staged performance, so you can rid yourself of associations with speeches as "anxiety-ridden performances." Moreover, thinking of the speech as communication keeps you focused on the audience, rather than on yourself, since your purpose is first and foremost to get your message across to them.

Have Faith in the Audience

Finally, keep in mind that the audience is on your side. Most people in the audience are sure to feel at least as anxious as you about public speaking, and they admire you for being at the podium. They are more interested in hearing what you have to say than in scrutinizing your presentation skills or counting how many times you say "um." Inexperienced speakers sometimes assume that the audience can easily detect their nervousness. But, if fact, researchers have learned that most people in the audience notice little or no anxiety in a speaker, especially if the content of the presentation is interesting and engaging. This result seems to be true even in speech classes, where the audience is particularly attuned to the speaker's presentation skills. Keep in mind that most of the time audiences cannot tell that you are nervous; they are not focusing on your anxiety. Unless you announce that you are nervous, or call attention to it with obvious indications of anxiety, the audience will be concentrating on your message, not your performance.

STRATEGIES FOR MANAGING ANXIETY *DURING* PRESENTATIONS

Now that we have covered some strategies that you can use while preparing and rehearsing your presentation, let's consider some things you can do to manage anxiety while actually presenting your speech.

Remember to Breathe

One invaluable piece of advice for public speaking is: "Remember to breathe!" Many people react to a stressful situation by tightening up physically and holding their breath, which physiologically adds to stress in the body as it craves more oxygen. Every relaxation and stress-reduction technique begins with breathing. Every athletic or performance activity stresses breathing as one of its "fundamentals" because breathing is the body's regulator.

Remember to breathe even before you stand up to speak. Take a few deep breaths and exhale slowly, while trying consciously to let go of the physical tension in your body as you breathe out. A useful yoga breathing technique is to retain your breath for a few seconds before you exhale; then breathe out slowly and deliberately, taking about twice as long to exhale as to inhale. The purpose of focusing on your breathing so closely is to establish a relaxed, regular breathing pattern that will help keep your voice and body under control. So before you actually begin to speak, take a moment to get set and focused, and to breathe. Then look at an interested person in the audience, smile, and begin your opening comments.

When planning your presentation be sure to build in pauses to breathe. Some students find it useful to write "REMEMBER TO BREATHE" on their note card or to pencil it in lightly in the margin of a flip chart. One business executive likes to pick out a pleasant-looking person in the audience and imagine that person is there specifically to remind her to breathe. Remember to practice using pauses to breathe when rehearsing your speech.

Set a Comfortable Speaking Pace

The speaking pace most people use for ordinary conversation is too fast for public speaking. So, most speakers need to slow down when presenting. But speaking more slowly makes some people self-conscious because they think they "don't sound like themselves" or because they feel their thoughts are getting ahead of their words. When rehearsing your speech, practice a speaking pace that makes you feel comfortable. If you catch yourself speeding up, pause to "reset" your speaking pace. You are probably talking too fast if you stumble over words, notice your sentences running together, or start to sound out of breath.

Be especially careful not to rush the introduction of your speech because that will set an uncomfortable pace for the rest of the presentation. It's a good strategy, in fact, to take extra time with your introduction or to include a humorous anecdote that will evoke a response from the audience, thus providing you an opportunity to pause. Time perception is often distorted during a presentation, so a one-second pause can feel like an eternity of "dead air." But short pauses do not seem interminable to the audience; in fact, pauses give the audience time to absorb information and follow your thoughts. So, when preparing your speech, look for places to *build in* pauses, particularly before you move on to a new point or a new visual.

It is fairly common for people to talk faster when they are nervous or excited, and you may find yourself speeding up even if you rehearsed your presentation at a comfortable pace. Some people speed up like a locomotive, building momentum, getting faster and faster as they go. In this situation it is important to put on the brakes as soon as you feel yourself getting out of control. Pause, take a breath, and reset your speaking pace. Remember, you are the engineer, and you control the locomotive's throttle.

Concentrate on One Point at a Time

As with most important tasks in life, it's good to deal with a presentation one step at a time. The time to worry about the organization and structure of your speech is during the preparation phase. That's the time to lay out your main points, exactly as you want to cover them and preferably using visual aids. Then, as you rehearse, you go over those main points until you literally "know them backwards and forwards." Thus when you present your speech, you don't need to worry about what's ahead. Concentrate on one point at a time, making each one as clear and interesting as you can, and making sure that the audience is following along. When you move to a new point, don't worry about what you already covered. Stay focused on "living in the present" with your speech. And at each new point you have an opportunity to pause and collect your thoughts before moving on.

Don't Dwell on Mistakes

Speech teachers and coaches recognize some patterns that occur with inexperienced public speakers. Here is one of them: a speaker begins a presentation with energy and enthusiasm, makes a good connection with the audience in the introduction, appears confident and relaxed, and then makes a small mistake, like mentioning one example out of order or stumbling over a word. Suddenly, the whole speech goes flat. The speaker's energy and confidence disappear; the connection with the audience breaks down. It is clear that the speaker has simply thrown in the towel and is now just going through the motions of "giving a speech."

This pattern often occurs with students who set their expectations too high. The best advice for the speaker in this scenario is this: "Your speech does not have to be perfect to be effective." Watch television news some evening and observe how often highly paid news anchors muff a line that they are *reading* from a teleprompter. You will see that even the pros are not perfect.

Our college recently invited a prominent Washington official, the director of an important federal agency, to speak as part of a Distinguished Lecture Series. He is a very polished and erudite public speaker. But at one point in his presentation he stumbled three times over the word "phenomenon," and finally paused and said offhandedly, "You know what I mean." Then he continued with his speech as if nothing unusual had happened. The mistake did not deflate him or damage his presentation. Speech students remembered that moment more than anything else he said or did because it showed them that even the best public speakers can make mistakes in a speech—even very obvious ones—and still be effective and look confident. What's important is not to dwell on a mistake, but to correct it

ANXIETY MONSTER

▼ Draw your anxiety monster below:

Charles Knapp
RVCC student

simply and straightforwardly, and move on. Remember, your speech does not have to be perfect to be effective! That advice helps many people maintain a healthy perspective about public speaking and provides a ready defense against the anxiety that arises when they think, "What if I make mistakes in my speech?"

Focus on the Audience, Not Yourself

Anxiety about public speaking sometimes feeds on itself when a speaker is so focused on his own nervousness that he becomes even more self-conscious and anxious. Such speakers are literally too much "into themselves." You cannot manage speech anxiety well if you continually dwell on it. The remedy is to focus *outward* on the audience, rather than *inward* on yourself. One effective technique is to think of a speech as a series of brief and informal conversations with individuals in the audience, rather than a lengthy, formal presentation to a large group. When you begin your introduction, look for friendly, attentive faces in the audience and make eye contact with these people. Imagine you are speaking with them one-on-one, at a casual lunch or over coffee, and discussing an issue that is important to you. As you continue the discussion, keep looking for other individuals to bring into the conversation. In this way, rather than feeling overwhelmed by a large, faceless audience, you will feel that you are interacting comfortably with familiar individuals.

Channel Energy Outward to the Audience

Finally, a useful strategy for dealing with speech anxiety is to channel your energy outward to the audience, to reach out physically to the audience. As the speaker, you are initiating a communication with these individuals, so it is your responsibility to engage them and hold their attention. If your posture and body language indicate that you are holding back or pulling away from them, your listeners will sense it and feel less connected with you. They may also pull away. Use broad, open gestures that show you want to extend yourself to your listeners and figuratively "embrace" them. Channeling energy outward can also help you release nervous tension in your body and animate your presentation, making you look enthusiastic and outgoing rather than agitated or jittery. Projecting energy outward can also help disguise some nervous behaviors, such as a shaky voice, stiff hands, or muscle tension in the upper body.

 **CONCLUSION**

The strategies and suggestions in this chapter have helped many people learn to manage their fear and anxiety about public speaking and become more accomplished speakers.

They can also help you, as they helped Michael, untie the knots that keep you from freeing the dynamic, confident speaker inside yourself.

Tips at a Glance for Managing Anxiety about Public Speaking

- Establish realistic expectations.
- Confront your fear.
- Make fear your ally.
- Commit yourself.
- Think positively.
- Prepare thoroughly.
- Imagine success.
- Practice relaxation.
- Focus on communication, not performance.
- Have faith in the audience.
- Remember to breathe.
- Set a comfortable speaking pace.
- Concentrate on one point at a time.
- Don't dwell on mistakes.
- Focus on the audience, not yourself.
- Channel energy outward to the audience.

ANXIETY MONSTER

▼ **Draw your anxiety monster below:**

CHAPTER 2

Getting Started

"Don't procrastinate. Select a topic and get down to work."

Eleanor, an independent consultant who specializes in effective time management, has accepted an invitation to speak for about ten minutes on a topic "in her field of interest" at a meeting of the Rotary Club in her community. She is accustomed to dealing with specific time management problems in big companies but is finding it difficult to choose a topic that would be interesting and appropriate for the diverse group of business and professional people in the Rotary. She is worried that her field of interest may be too specialized and theoretical for the audience. She doesn't want to talk over their heads or bore them. So Eleanor calls the president of the organization to find out more about current goals and concerns of the Rotary, and about topics other speakers have addressed at their meetings. She also calls a friend who belongs to the Rotary and chats with him about the stalwarts of the organization and their interests. She asks herself what these people would want to learn from her experience with time management. She wants to speak about something practical that could really help Rotary members improve their everyday lives.

With this purpose in mind Eleanor writes out a list of possible topics and decides the most promising one is "how to make the most of your leisure time." However, she realizes that most of the people in her audience are very active in business and community affairs and do not have a lot of leisure. Suddenly, Eleanor hits upon the perfect topic, one that she knows the Rotary will remember and greatly appreciate: "how to create more leisure time in your busy life."

 # SELECTING A TOPIC

For many students the hardest part about getting started on a speech is choosing a topic. Some people have so much trouble selecting a topic that they ask to be assigned one. But finding an appropriate topic for a speech is an important part of the presentation process because you cannot expect to make a speech meaningful for the audience unless the topic is first meaningful to you. Audiences respond not only to the content of a speech, but also to the interest and enthusiasm of the speaker. You have better chances for an effective speech if the audience can sense your enthusiasm for the topic. Following are some suggestions that can help you select a topic that will be meaningful for you and the audience.

Start with What You Know

Every human being has knowledge, experiences, and memories that make her or him unique. An experience that one person considers mundane may be very interesting, even exotic, to another person. That's why there are so many popular expressions like "One man's junk is another man's treasure." So, when selecting a topic always start with what you know. Everyone has some special area of interest or expertise; all you have to do is discover what that is. If you are at a loss, make a list of your interests that might be worth sharing with other people. For example, if you have lived or traveled extensively in another country, look for a presentation topic that can incorporate your first-hand experience or perspective of that country. On the other hand, you might also find an interesting topic in ordinary, everyday experience. If you sell athletic shoes, for example, you may be uniquely qualified to talk about "how to buy sneakers that fit your training needs and your budget."

Look Where You Invest Your Time and Energy

If you don't want to make an inventory of your interests and activities to find a topic, look closely at those that are most important to you. Where do you invest most of your time and energy? What do you like to do? What are you passionate about? Like Eleanor, you may find a good topic in your field of work or study. Or you may find it in leisure activities—sports, hobbies, clubs and social organizations, political or environmental activism, community service, or anything else you do just for the love of it. Don't undervalue your experience or "expertise" in activities you are passionate about. You often do not need special credentials to speak on your personal interests. If you have tried scuba diving one time, you are not an expert compared with the dive master, but for an audience of people who have never tried scuba you have enough credibility for a presentation about recreational diving.

Brainstorm Ideas

Brainstorming is a technique for generating many ideas quickly. It can be effective for both individuals and small groups. To brainstorm a speech topic you would try to write down as many ideas as you can for a speech in a short time, say within five or ten minutes. There are several effective ways to brainstorm. Some people write lists, as Eleanor did, to generate possible topics. Others prefer to *free write* whatever thoughts and associations come to mind about a particular subject. What's important about brainstorming is to avoid evaluating or critiquing the ideas you generate. There will be time to sort through them and evaluate them later. Brainstorming is tapping into your unconscious creativity, into the stream of free-flowing images and ideas in your mind. The point is not to inhibit this flow in any way.

Use Mind Mapping

A currently popular brainstorming technique is *mind mapping,* or *concept mapping,* popularized by Tony Buzan in *The Mind Map Book.* Mind mapping is a process for generating ideas and identifying relationships among them. Unlike outlining, mind mapping promotes nonlinear thinking that uncovers connections among ideas that may not be apparent at first. Mind mapping can be a simple paper-and-pencil process or, with mind-mapping software, an easy-to-use computer program that can help you generate a speech topic. You start with one main idea in the center of a blank page and try to identify other related ideas that "radiate" like spokes from the main idea, drawing lines to connect them with the main idea and with each other. Figure 2.1 illustrates a mind map created to generate ideas for an informative presentation about cheetahs. (See Chapter 8 for a full discussion of the process of developing this speech.) Some ideas on the mind map may not end up in the speech, but including a lot of them will provide more options to plan with. A mind map should help the speaker discover connections among the most important ideas about the topic, and eventually provide some structure for the presentation's content.

Browse the Internet

If you already have a general idea for a speech topic, you can focus it more by browsing Internet websites on your subject. Browsing helps you learn more about the topic quickly and gives you a head start on research for a speech by lining up potentially important resources you can bookmark and draw upon later. Of course, to focus your topic you can also browse through other information resources, such as books, magazines, journals, and newspapers.

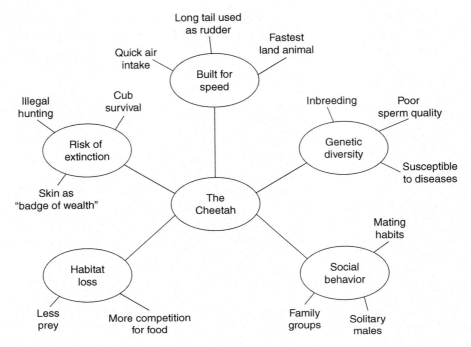

FIGURE 2.1

Look for Controversy

Some of the best speeches, especially persuasive speeches, spring from controversy. We live in an age when people are inundated with information and confronted with controversial issues in so many areas of their lives. If you can clarify one of these issues for your audience, you will be doing them a service. Looking for controversy does not mean that you have to take on major hot-button issues such as abortion, gun control, or capital punishment. In fact, it's usually better to avoid such highly volatile issues on which most people have already made up their minds. On the other hand, people are more likely to change their opinion, or to form one, if you raise their consciousness about issues and problems that affect their everyday lives. Look around your school, workplace, or community for issues with a touch of controversy. Talk about the pros and cons of dress-down days in the office, for example, or effective ways to deter campus litterbugs, or good reasons to participate in an upcoming community blood drive.

 NARROWING THE TOPIC

A common problem for inexperienced speakers is selecting a topic that is too general. A speech can seem like such a daunting project at the outset that people are sometimes afraid that they will not have enough to talk about. Consequently, they opt for topics that are too broad. But it is actually more difficult and time consuming to research a broad topic than a narrow one because the broader the topic, the more information there is to gather and sort. Moreover, a broad topic is often inherently less interesting than a specific one. For example, which of these two presentations sounds more interesting to you: a presentation entitled "Physical and Behavioral Characteristics of the Humpback Whale," or one entitled "The Humpback Whale: Singin' in the Waves," specifically about communication behaviors among humpbacks?

When selecting your speech topic, define it as specifically as you can in the beginning, and then continue to narrow it down as you work with it. Eleanor recognized that her original topic was too broad for a ten-minute presentation. By narrowing the topic, Eleanor ensures not only that her speech will fit the allotted time but also that it will better address the specific needs and concerns of her audience.

 ## STATING THE PURPOSE

After selecting a topic, the next important step in getting started with a speech is to determine why you are giving the speech and what you expect the audience to get from it. To do this you need to write a *purpose statement,* which is one declarative sentence stating exactly what you want your audience to know, believe, or do after hearing your speech. (For persuasive presentations the purpose statement is usually called the *proposition.* See Chapter 10.) A clear purpose statement is important for focusing and shaping your speech. Noted author and communication consultant Dianna Booher says, "If you can't write your message in a sentence, you can't say it in an hour."

Eleanor's speech to the Rotary did not begin to take shape until she settled on its purpose. Eleanor ultimately decided on this purpose statement for her presentation to the Rotary:

> *"I want to persuade the audience to follow five basic principles of time management that can help them create more leisure time in their busy lives."*

This purpose statement is clear, specific, and realistic for a ten-minute speech. To appreciate its clarity, consider the following purpose statement for a speech about children and television:

> *"I want to explain the impact of television on children."*

This purpose statement is much too general, unfocused, and unrealistic. What does the phrase "the impact of television" mean? Does it refer to programming or advertising? Cartoons or game shows? Is this impact positive or negative? Is the impact on the children's eye sight, their social behavior, their performance in school? Books would need to be written to accomplish this purpose! Here are two ways this flawed purpose statement might be refocused to produce one that is more specific and more realistic:

> *"I want to explain the beneficial impact of* Sesame Street *on the social interaction of children in kindergarten."*

> *"I want to persuade the audience that violent cartoons on television encourage hyperactivity among preschool boys."*

For more help in developing the purpose statement for your speech use the "Purpose Statement Worksheet" at the end of the chapter.

 # RESEARCHING THE TOPIC

Sources of Information

Much of your credibility as a speaker depends on the quality of the information, examples, and evidence you present. Sometimes, like Eleanor, you may already know quite a lot about your topic. But more often you will need to research your topic as you prepare your speech. Even if you already know your topic, it is good practice to check on new developments in your field to ensure your information is current and generally refresh your memory. Moreover, researching your topic will help you feel more secure and confident about the presentation.

For speeches, as for any research project, you can draw upon conventional resources: books, periodicals, databases, the Internet. There are many good research guides that explain how to use these resources effectively, and for specific research problems you should ask a reference librarian for help.

But, depending on your topic, there are other less conventional resources that you may wish to draw upon for your speech—for example, documentary or commercial films, radio or television broadcasts, YouTube videos, blogs or Internet chat rooms, travel brochures, business prospectuses, annual reports, medical studies, racing forms, program or liner notes, exhibition catalogues, museum lectures, magazine ads, junk mail, architectural floor plans, and so forth. So, be imaginative and resourceful about researching information for your speech.

Interviews can be particularly valuable sources of information for speeches. There may be a gold mine of information, experience, and expertise only a phone call or an e-mail message away. For example, if you are preparing a presentation on the advantages of radio advertising for small businesses, you will likely learn more about demographics and advertising rates by telephoning local radio stations than by visiting the public library. The point is that if you can locate "an expert" to interview for your speech, you will make the presentation a much richer experience both for yourself and your audience.

Evaluating Sources

One problem with using unconventional resources is that it is often difficult to evaluate how accurate and reliable their information is. Uncle George's recollections of his service as a fire jumper may be faded or exaggerated; the travel agency's brochures may be incomplete or outdated; blog and chat room comments may be heavily biased or narrowminded. Reliability of information is especially problematic today with the Internet. You can find websites that state unequivocally that the United States won the Vietnam War, that the Holocaust never took place, or that Elvis Presley has been sighted recently in Uruguay. How are we supposed to determine when such information is credible and when it is not? Keep in mind these basic considerations about information on the Internet:

- **Anyone can put information on a website.** Can you identify the author? Can you determine the author's credentials?

- **Sources of information on the Internet are sometimes unclear.** Are there citations or annotations to indicate where the information comes from?

- **Information on the Internet is often not in its original form.** Can you determine if the information has been edited, quoted out of context, or altered (intentionally or unintentionally) in some way?

- **Information on the Internet is not systematically reviewed or evaluated.** Unlike scholarly books and articles, there is not an established review process whereby information on the Internet is evaluated by experts, editors, or publishers. Can you determine if the information comes from a reputable institution, such as a university, a credible media organization, or a recognized institution?

For information from the Internet the best rule of thumb is one that every responsible journalist follows: Always check and recheck your sources. On the home page of most libraries you can find links to reputable Web resources or "Best of the Internet" sites in various academic areas. Many libraries also post online guidelines for evaluating Internet information or for catching "warning signs" that the information may not be reliable or credible.

Finally, here is one other valuable piece of advice about researching your speech. Research can be very time consuming. At the beginning, you cannot know how long it will take to find good material for your presentation, or how long it might take to get your hands on it. Ordering books or articles through interlibrary loan, for example, may take several weeks. Setting up an interview with an "expert" may require more lead time than you expect. It is always best to start your research early; don't procrastinate. Often the real enemy of a successful presentation is not anxiety, but procrastination.

DEVELOPING AND ORGANIZING THE SPEECH

Once you have defined a topic and written a purpose statement—the foundations of your speech—you are ready to build on them and develop the structure of your speech. By this time you probably already know many of the main points and examples you want to use in the speech. Now it is time to sort through them and organize a cohesive presentation.

Outlining

Although there is no definitive way to put together a speech, certain essential elements must fall into place for a presentation to be unified and cohesive. A speech needs to have a *central idea,* sometimes called a *thesis,* to which everything in the speech relates; several *main points* that develop the central idea; and *evidence* and *examples* that support and illustrate the main points. The thesis of Eleanor's persuasive speech to the Rotary is:

> *If you follow five simple principles of time management, you will become more efficient and create more leisure time for yourself.*

The main points for this speech will obviously be the five principles of time management that Eleanor wants to present. The examples used to explain and illustrate these main points are important because they largely determine how well the audience will remember and accept her recommendations about time management. Eleanor should choose examples that will convince the audience that the principles apply specifically to them.

Organizational Patterns

There are many different ways to organize information and arguments for a speech. Here in a nutshell are five common organizational patterns and some suggestions on how to use them:

- *Chronological.* Be an historian. Draw a time line. Show a sequence of events leading up to the present situation. Show the influence of the past on the present.
- *Spatial.* Be an architect or a stage director. Use a diagram or a blueprint. Show how the physical parts fit together. Show the impact of physical changes on specific locations.
- *Comparison/Contrast.* Be an educator or a salesperson. Use slides or models. Show before and after, pros and cons, advantages and disadvantages.
- *Cause-and-Effect.* Be a pollster or a market researcher. Present charts, graphs, and spreadsheets as evidence. Show the germs that cause the illness, the ads that sell the product, the exercises that reduce the fat.
- *Problem/Solution.* Be an advocate or a reformer. Present photographs or fabric samples as exhibits. Show what to do about declining sales, local water shortages, environmental hazards.

Organizing with Visual Aids

You may have noticed that for each of the organizational patterns just listed there is a hint about how you might incorporate visual aids, a good practice to follow for any speech you present. Visual aids can help you shape and structure material for a speech. One useful strategy is to organize a presentation around the headings on visual aids. These headings will be the main points of your speech outline, and the bullet points under the headings will be the supporting evidence and examples. Figures 2.2 through 2.8 provide examples of this organizational strategy using PowerPoint slides for a problem/solution speech about hearing loss caused by overexposure to noise in our daily lives. Notice that the slide headings for the body of the speech by themselves present a complete outline for the speech topic and lay out the five main concerns that the speaker intends to address. They provide basic physiological information about our hearing organs in Figure 2.3, set up the dangers to our hearing (the *problem*) in Figures 2.4 and 2.5, and list precautions for preventing hearing loss (the *solution*) in Figures 2.6 and 2.7. The bullet points on these slides introduce the speaker's supporting information, data, and evidence. All she needs to supply are examples and personal experience to flesh out the presentation. (See Chapter 5 for a complete discussion of how to prepare and use visual aids, including more suggestions for how to organize a presentation around A/V headings.)

 ANALYZING THE AUDIENCE

After you have decided on the message for your speech, you must consider the audience who will receive it. The best speeches are prepared for a specific audience in a specific setting. Consequently, experienced speakers try to learn as much as they can about their audience before and during the presentation.

Getting to Know Your Audience *before* the Speech

Getting to know your audience *before* the speech means gathering as much pertinent information as you can about the group itself and how it can benefit from your presentation. If you know who the audience is, you can avoid covering what they already know or alienating them inadvertently with a disagreeable comment or attitude. You can find the right range for your comments, where you neither talk down to the audience nor over their heads. Knowing the audience does not mean that you only try to affirm what they already believe; it means you may be able to challenge their beliefs in terms they will understand and appreciate.

As you prepare your presentation, you need to consider your audience's particular needs and interests. The "Audience Analysis Checklist" at the end of this chapter outlines the kind of questions you should ask about your audience before the speech. Not all the

FIGURE 2.2

Magic School Bus Tour!

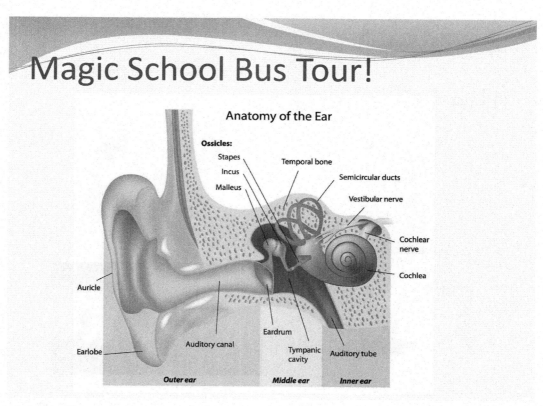

FIGURE 2.3

The Price We Pay

FIGURE 2.4

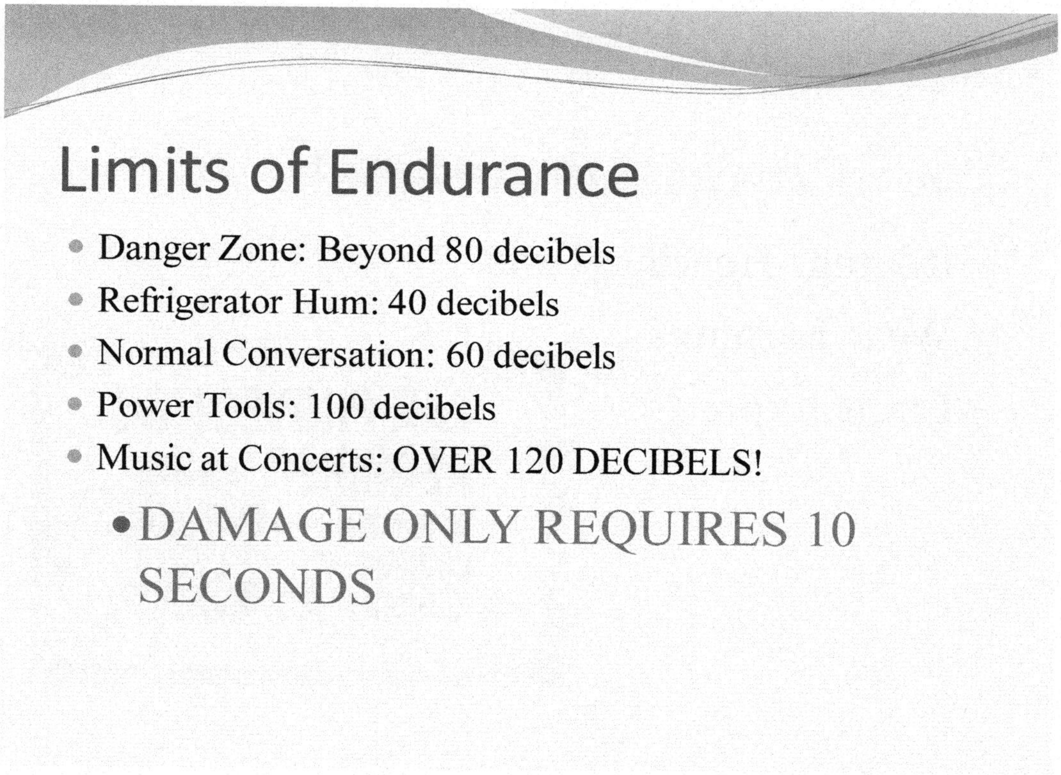

Limits of Endurance

- Danger Zone: Beyond 80 decibels
- Refrigerator Hum: 40 decibels
- Normal Conversation: 60 decibels
- Power Tools: 100 decibels
- Music at Concerts: OVER 120 DECIBELS!

  - DAMAGE ONLY REQUIRES 10 SECONDS

FIGURE 2.5

Your Protective Arsenal

- Regular Hearing Tests
- Wear Earplugs
- Limit Exposure

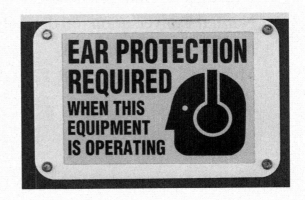

FIGURE 2.6

Your Protective Arsenal (cont.)

FIGURE 2.7

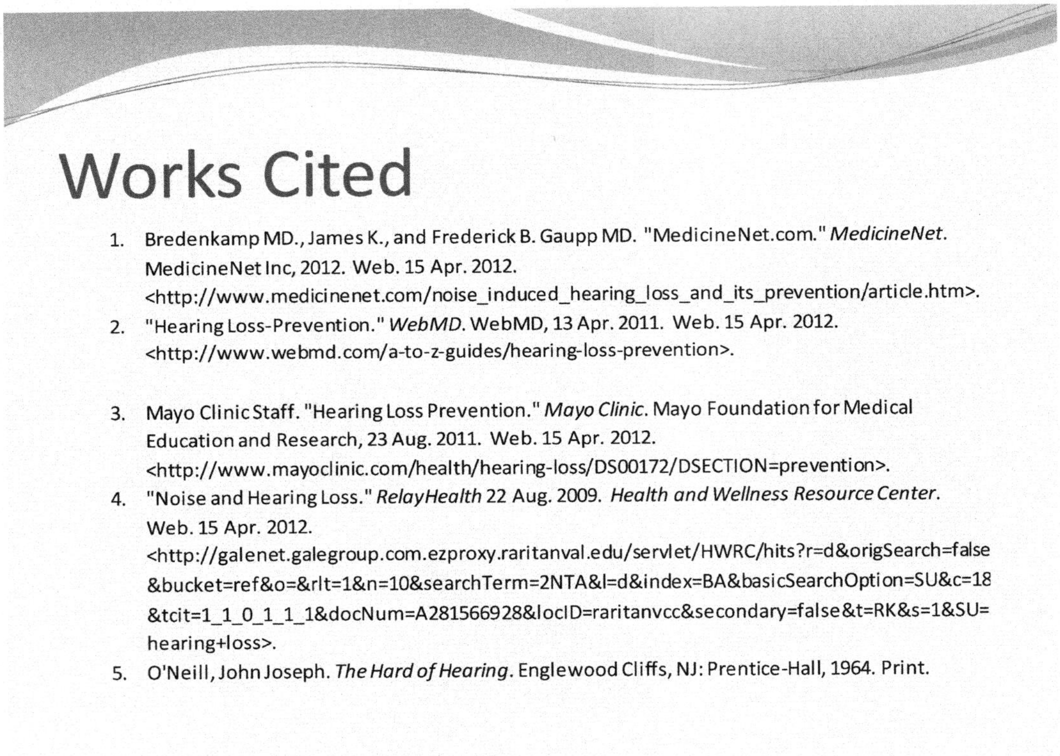

Works Cited

1. Bredenkamp MD., James K., and Frederick B. Gaupp MD. "MedicineNet.com." *MedicineNet*. MedicineNet Inc, 2012. Web. 15 Apr. 2012. <http://www.medicinenet.com/noise_induced_hearing_loss_and_its_prevention/article.htm>.
2. "Hearing Loss-Prevention." *WebMD*. WebMD, 13 Apr. 2011. Web. 15 Apr. 2012. <http://www.webmd.com/a-to-z-guides/hearing-loss-prevention>.

3. Mayo Clinic Staff. "Hearing Loss Prevention." *Mayo Clinic*. Mayo Foundation for Medical Education and Research, 23 Aug. 2011. Web. 15 Apr. 2012. <http://www.mayoclinic.com/health/hearing-loss/DS00172/DSECTION=prevention>.
4. "Noise and Hearing Loss." *RelayHealth* 22 Aug. 2009. *Health and Wellness Resource Center*. Web. 15 Apr. 2012. <http://galenet.galegroup.com.ezproxy.raritanval.edu/servlet/HWRC/hits?r=d&origSearch=false&bucket=ref&o=&rlt=1&n=10&searchTerm=2NTA&l=d&index=BA&basicSearchOption=SU&c=18&tcit=1_1_0_1_1_1&docNum=A281566928&locID=raritanvcc&secondary=false&t=RK&s=1&SU=hearing+loss>.
5. O'Neill, John Joseph. *The Hard of Hearing*. Englewood Cliffs, NJ: Prentice-Hall, 1964. Print.

FIGURE 2.8

questions may apply for your speech, but many of them are relevant for any public speaking situation. For example, you should try to learn about demographics that define your audience, their basic values and beliefs, and what they already know about your topic. You should also try to figure out what they *need* to know and *want* to know about you topic, as well as what they may be likely to question or challenge in your presentation.

Also included at the end of the chapter is a "Student Audience Analysis Questionnaire," designed specifically to help students in speech classes and presentation skills workshops find out how much their classmates already know about a speech topic, what they do and do not want to hear about it, and how the topic might best be presented for them.

Getting to Know Your Audience *during* the Speech

Getting to know your audience during the speech is sometimes even more important than audience analysis before the speech. At the time of the presentation you can observe who they actually are and find out what they think about your topic. You may have an opportunity to meet and speak with some audience members on site before your presentation. And during your presentation keep in mind that your audience is also communicating with you, reacting nonverbally to your ideas, and often revealing what they think or feel about them. You will be able to take advantage of this audience feedback if you really look at people and notice whether they are interested, puzzled, bored, hesitant, or excited about your ideas.

For example, the speaker who prepared the presentation about preventing hearing loss already has a great deal of personal experience and credibility with this topic. But she may have to decide, depending on the audience's previous experience with this topic (or lack of it), how much to disclose about her own hearing loss or how much time to spend on the physiology of hearing. Therefore, it will be important for her to gauge—either beforehand or with well-placed questions early in her speech—what the audience already knows about her topic. And she may even have to decide about simple details in her speech, such as whether the audience members will already know what "decibels" are or whether they will understand the reference in her title to an "Inconvenient Truth." Experienced speakers are able to make small adjustments in their presentations as they gauge audience reactions. For example, they may sense that people need an additional example to grasp a concept, or conversely, that they have grasped the point immediately and are ready for a new one. If you pay attention to nonverbal feedback from individuals in the audience, you can often anticipate questions or objections that might come up in a discussion or question-and-answer session and, therefore, address them more thoroughly in the presentation.

As mentioned in Chapter 1, speaking to individuals in the audience is also a good strategy for managing anxiety about public speaking. By seeing the audience as individual people, rather than an amorphous group, you will feel more at ease with them and the audience will seem a lot less scary.

CONCLUSION

Almost everyone feels a bit overwhelmed when faced with an important speech or an oral report. And sometimes just getting started is the hardest part. This chapter has laid out some practical steps you can follow to get your speech rolling. It is appropriate that the opening scenario for this chapter relates to a speech about time management because getting off to a good start with a speech is essentially a matter of effective time management. Don't procrastinate; get down to work. Choose a topic and state your purpose as soon as you can. Research information about your topic and your audience, and organize your speech. The sooner you get started, the better are the chances that your speech will be one the audience will remember and take to heart.

TIPS AT A GLANCE FOR GETTING STARTED

- Don't procrastinate! Get started as soon as possible.
- Select a topic that will be meaningful both to you and to your audience.
- State the purpose of your presentation clearly and succinctly.
- Research your topic thoroughly.
- Organize and develop your presentation using headings and bullets points for visual aids.
- Get to know your audience beforehand and during the presentation.

PURPOSE STATEMENT WORKSHEET

1. Write in one declarative sentence (subject > verb > object) the main idea you want the audience to remember after you have finished your speech.

For example: Computers will solve your billing deficit.

Not: I will discuss computers and what they can do for you.

2. Look at the sentence you wrote and ask these three questions:

• Do you have a subject and only one subject?

E.g.: Effective computer usage will save you money.

Not: The history of computers and their present usage will show you why you need them now. (You could write three speeches from this sentence.)

• Do you take a definite stand on the subject?

E.g.: Computers will save your company $10 million a year.

Not: Computers? Will they help? (Don't ask. Tell.)

• Do you use clear, concrete, precise words?

E.g.: Changing your computer system now will save you $10 million next year.

Not: In the near future, your company will be much happier if you change your computer system now. (Say it straight out!)

3. Revise your purpose statement to fit these three criteria. Now write it in one straight-forward sentence.

AUDIENCE ANALYSIS CHECKLIST

Audience Profile

- What kind of audience is it? (general audience, college class, youth group, charitable organization, business association, club, etc.)
- Does the group have a name? (Junior Chamber of Commerce, Environmental Action Club, St. Margaret's CYO, etc.)
- Do I know someone in this group or someone who has experience with it?
- Is my speech part of a special occasion this group celebrates or commemorates? (founder's day ceremonies, academic awards luncheon, annual business meeting, etc.)
- How can I connect my personal experience with this group?
- How can I compliment this audience?
- How large is the audience?
- What demographics define this audience? (average age, socioeconomic background, educational level, professional interests, etc.)
- What is this audience likely to know about my topic already?

Audience Attitudes

- What attitude is this audience likely to have about my topic? (enthusiastic, positive, neutral, averse, negative, hostile, etc.)
- What is most likely to interest this audience about my topic?
- What does this audience most want or need to know about my topic?
- What kind of information, examples, or research references would be most influential with this audience?
- What would this audience most likely question or challenge about my presentation?
- How can I best establish speaker credibility with this audience?
- What kind of visual aids would be most effective with this audience?
- What questions would this audience likely ask about my topic in the discussion or question-and-answer session?

Presentation Setting

- What kind of speaking situation is it? (classroom or business presentation, panel discussion, awards luncheon, commencement speech, keynote address, eulogy, etc.)
- Are there other speakers on the program? If so, where do I fit in?

- What is the setting for the speech? (classroom, auditorium, banquet hall, business meeting room, church basement, etc.)
- How large is the room?
- How are the acoustics and sightlines in the room?
- How is lighting in the room? Can it be adjusted or controlled?
- How is the podium equipped? (desk, lectern, microphone, whiteboard, easel stand, etc.)
- What are the room's technological capabilities? (DVD player, LCD projector, wireless Internet connection, etc.)
- Are there any potential problems or distractions related to the setting? (possible interruptions, noise from another room, heating/cooling or ventilation equipment, computer malfunctions, etc.)
- Are there any problems or special considerations related to the timing of the speech? (late evening, immediately after lunch, close to quitting time, a holiday, an anniversary of a special event, etc.)

STUDENT AUDIENCE ANALYSIS QUESTIONNAIRE

Speech topic: _____

Ask each person in your group the following questions. Take notes on this page.

- How much do you already know about my speech topic?

1	**2**	**3**	**4**
Nothing	**Not much**	**Fairly much**	**Very much**

- If you answered 1 or 2, what would you like to know, specifically?

- If you answered 3 or 4, how can I make this speech interesting for you?

- How can I make this topic more relevant or engaging for you?

- What *don't* you want to hear about this topic? Why?

Developing Introductions
and Conclusions

"Your introduction and conclusion are golden opportunities
for making a powerful impact on your audience."

Jason has great material for a persuasive speech about the dangers of lawn tractors. His research has turned up startling statistics about the number of accidents that occur with them, as well as some compelling quotations from public safety officials. And, best of all, he has a dramatic personal experience to relate about an accident with a lawn tractor he suffered as a child. Yet with all this dramatic material to grab the audience's attention and set up his topic, Jason opens his speech very undramatically with this bland introduction:

> *Good afternoon. Today I would like to talk to you about the dangers*
> *of lawn tractors. You probably don't have much interest in riding*
> *mowers and don't realize how dangerous they can be.*

Inexperienced speakers have a tendency to announce their topic to the audience as soon as they begin speaking. Unfortunately, Jason gave in to this tendency and wasted an excellent opportunity to create a dynamic first impression of himself and his message about lawn tractors.

Consider how the audience might react to Jason's opening comments for this speech. There may be some people in the audience who think that, given all the really serious problems in the world, the dangers of lawn tractors is a pretty frivolous topic. Jason has lost these people. There may be others who say to themselves, "I don't have a riding lawn mower; this doesn't apply to me." And they tune out. Those wavering about whether to give Jason their attention may also tune out because he has already planted the suggestion in their minds that they "probably don't have much interest in riding mowers."

But consider the effect Jason might have on this audience with this revised introduction:

> *I will never forget the day before my fifth birthday. My father was sprucing up the yard for my big birthday party the next afternoon. All my friends were coming, and I was pretty excited. As he cruised around the backyard on his lawn tractor, he called out, "Hop on, I'll take you for a spin." That was exciting too because I loved to ride with him on that huge, powerful lawn mower. But as he made a sharp turn around a newly planted white pine, the mower bumped over a rock and I was thrown off my father's lap. Before he could stop the mower, the blade ran over my foot, shredded my sneaker, and sliced off two toes.*
>
> *According to the American National Safety Council, several thousand accidents like this occur in our country every year, and almost all of them can be easily prevented. Today I'd like to inform you about the dangers of lawn tractors and suggest a few basic precautions that can prevent senseless accidents like the one that spoiled my fifth birthday.*

By relating his unfortunate personal experience with the mower *before* announcing the topic of his speech Jason creates an entirely different impression of himself and his message. This introduction is far more effective because Jason's story engages the audience and sets up his credibility before they have a chance to tune out. Even people who may not be especially interested in this topic will pay attention to Jason because his distressing personal experience arouses interest and evokes an emotional reaction to the dangers of lawn tractors.

This chapter is about developing effective introductions and conclusions for your presentations. The introduction and conclusion to your speech can have a powerful impact on the audience, perhaps greater than all the rest of your presentation. Unlike most public speaking textbooks, which typically cover introductions and conclusions within a chapter about organizing and developing a speech, *The Confident Speaker's Handbook* devotes this entire chapter to introductions and conclusions because they are so important to an effective presentation. There is an old Vaudeville adage: "Know how to get on, know how to get off, and the rest will take care of itself." This chapter will help you "get on" and "get off" well with your presentation and make a lasting impression on your audience.

GUIDELINES FOR EFFECTIVE INTRODUCTIONS

An effective introduction is a fairly complex piece of work and requires careful preparation. A good introduction is not just a casual "warm-up" for the body of a speech, but rather a separate mini-speech that has to accomplish several critical functions in a short time. A good introduction has to get the audience's attention, establish speaker credibility, and introduce the topic.

Getting the Audience's Attention

Research shows that in short speeches audiences are most likely to remember the introduction. In longer speeches they are more likely to remember the conclusion. On the other hand, if a longer speech does not get the audience's attention early on, there may not be many engaged listeners left at the end to remember the conclusion.

Experienced speakers always look for imaginative ways to grab the audience's attention right at the beginning of a speech. Like savvy advertisers, they know that they have to make their message stand out immediately. Here are some effective attention-getting techniques you can use in your introduction:

- **Tell an anecdote.** Make it dramatic, personal, or humorous. Audiences enjoy and remember interesting stories. For example, in his revised introduction Jason uses his personal experience to dramatize the dangers of lawn tractors.

- **Pose a question.** Whether real or rhetorical, a good opening question helps involve the audience personally and gets them thinking about your topic before you actually introduce it. "How many of you have thought about what you really want from a vacation?" It is important to follow up a question and guide the audience closer to the heart of your topic. For example: "Most of us think of a vacation as a time to 'get away' from a job or a routine, but what do we want to get away *to?*" Be careful not to let a question become just another way of announcing your topic. "How many of you have been to Helsinki?" is not a scintillating opening question for a presentation about Finland. If the drift of your presentation depends on the answer to that question, work it into the introduction later.

- **Use a startling statistic.** In our number-crunching society, statistics (if they are not overused or too difficult to comprehend) usually make a strong impression on audiences. "Recent medical studies indicate that more than 50 percent of American teenagers, because of poor diet and lack of exercise, already show evidence of early stages of cardiovascular disease."

- **Quote an authority.** State what a famous person or recognized expert has said about your topic. There are reference books and websites with famous quotations on any subject. President John F. Kennedy's famous comment, "Ask not what your country can do for you, but what you can do for your country," might be a good opener for a speech about community service.

- **Make a provocative statement.** Stir up the audience with a comment that is likely to provoke a strong reaction. "Citizens of most industrialized countries consider Americans who do not speak a foreign language unsophisticated and boorish."

- **Put the audience in the picture.** Use details and examples to draw the audience into a specific problem or event, as Jason did with his mower accident. Or create a hypothetical situation that you ask the audience to imagine.

- **Reveal something personal.** Audiences usually feel privileged or flattered to be let in on something personal about the speaker. Jason's childhood experience with the mower is a good example. Revealing something personal does not mean you have to divulge intimate secrets. Advice a favorite teacher once gave you or a humorous remark your baby sister made about your topic may be personal enough.

- **Demonstrate something interesting or unusual.** "Show," rather than "tell," how a diabetic tests her blood sugar level, how a police officer handcuffs a suspected criminal, how a wood carver handles a chisel.

- **Juxtapose opposites for dramatic effect.** "In death, we can give new life. It sounds paradoxical, but it's true. By donating your organs you can provide others with a chance for a healthy and normal life."

- **Use a clever visual.** For a presentation on credit card abuse among college students, entitled "Don't Get Hooked on Credit Cards," a marketing student backed up her introduction with a PowerPoint slide showing an image of a fisherman with credit cards on a large hook.

Establishing the Speaker's Credibility

The second critical function of an effective introduction is to establish the speaker's credibility. The word *credibility* comes from the Latin verb *credere,* which means "to believe." Credibility is all about why the audience should believe what you say. For your speech to be successful you must somehow convince the audience to accept your message.

For many formal presentations a master of ceremonies introduces the featured speaker and presents her credentials, or qualifications, to speak about the topic at hand. This takes much of the burden of establishing credibility off the speaker's shoulders, although it is still important for the speaker to reinforce her credibility in the introduction. But how does the speaker establish credibility if no one introduces her? Should she wave diplomas and certificates at the audience? Highlight her résumé? Mention her accomplishments? Fortunately, since most people are reluctant to "blow their own horn" in public, there are more subtle ways a speaker can establish credibility for a presentation. Here are some of them:

- **Describe relevant personal experience.** Show that "you've been there" already. This is primarily how Jason establishes credibility for his speech on mower safety. The fact that he lost two toes in a mower accident certainly qualifies him to speak on this subject. However, personal experience doesn't necessarily have to be firsthand, like Jason's, to be convincing. If you were Jason's neighbor or a classmate, or if even hearing about his accident affected you deeply, you could use those secondhand connections with Jason's experience to establish your own credibility for a talk about lawn tractor safety.

- **Don't undervalue or overlook your credentials.** One student preparing an informative speech on sky diving lined up a few colorful anecdotes about the sport for his introduction. But he didn't originally plan to mention that he started his "jump career" as an Army Ranger, and that after the service he made more than eighty sky dives and was about to receive an instructor's rating. Needless to say, his credibility on the topic of sky diving rose to new levels when he added this information into his introduction.

- **Show that you are passionate about your topic.** Even if you do not have extensive personal experience related to your topic, you can often establish credibility if you show the audience that you are passionate about it. For speeches on topics such as environmental issues, health and fitness, self-improvement, public safety, or volunteerism, speakers can usually establish their credibility by demonstrating an enthusiastic attitude.

- **Show that you have researched the topic.** For any presentation, and especially persuasive speeches, the audience needs to see that you "have done your homework." You should always present supporting data and arguments in the body of the speech, of course. But to establish credibility early on you should also show in the introduction that you have researched your topic, and that you are well prepared to speak on it. Jason does this by including a statistic on mower accidents from a recognized authority, the American National Safety Council. Citing this one source in the introduction indicates to the audience that Jason knows this topic, not only from first-hand personal experience, but also from researching it.

Introducing the Topic

The third important function of an effective introduction is to introduce the topic. To introduce the topic means more than to *announce* the topic, which is what Jason did in his original introduction. Notice that in the revised introduction Jason says he will talk about "the *dangers* of lawn tractors" and also suggest "simple *precautions*" to prevent mower accidents. He is not only introducing the presentation's two main ideas and but also indicating its overall structure and organization. Attentive listeners will recognize from the outset that this will be a two-part *problem/solution* speech.

Introducing the topic effectively also means that the speaker connects the topic with the audience. Just because Jason has been traumatized by a lawn tractor accident does not mean that the audience will automatically identify or connect with that experience. It is the speaker's responsibility to establish that connection. In the last sentence of his introduction Jason states the purpose of his presentation, to "inform" about the dangers of lawn tractors and "suggest" a few precautions that can prevent senseless accidents. This *purpose statement* connects the audience with Jason's presentation because Jason's knowledge and experience can protect others, including his listeners, from suffering a similar accident.

An introduction that sets up the topic effectively can serve as a blueprint for the rest of the speech. The more detailed the blueprint, the easier it is to develop the body of the speech and make all the parts fit together. For example, if Jason wanted to develop visual aids for this presentation on lawn tractors, two obvious headings would be "Dangers" and "Precautions." Once he identifies these headings, Jason can line up bullets to discuss under each heading and organize his information to support each point. His speech will practically write itself.

Also notice that Jason introduces the topic of his speech as the last element of the introduction, which provides a natural segue to the body of the speech. When organizing your presentation, try to address the three functions of a good introduction in the order presented here: first get the audience's attention, then establish credibility, and finally introduce the topic.

One final lesson to draw from the introduction to Jason's speech is the importance of *revising*. Jason's original introduction does more damage than good for his presentation. But his revised introduction is a blueprint for an outstanding speech. Don't settle for a mediocre, lackluster introduction. Personalize it, dramatize it, and make it specific. And don't be afraid to overhaul a weak introduction completely. Remember, your introduction will largely determine whether the audience buys into your message.

TIPS FOR DELIVERING THE INTRODUCTION

For most people the nervousness they feel about public speaking manifests itself immediately before and right at the beginning of a speech. All the eyes staring, all the facts and information to remember, all the delivery skills to keep track of can overwhelm a speaker during the crucial first minute of a presentation. Nervous behaviors, such as awkward body posture, shuffling feet, jingling loose change, or coughing and clearing the throat, can be especially troublesome at the beginning of a speech. Some speakers even call attention to their nervousness or insecurity by announcing to the audience that they feel uneasy or unprepared to speak. If you have put a lot of effort into preparing an effective introduction for your speech, you do not want to undermine that effort with shoddy delivery. Here are some tips to help you present your introduction to best advantage:

- **Rehearse your introduction separately.** Think of the introduction (also the conclusion) as independent from the body of the speech and rehearse it separately.

- **Memorize your opening remarks.** Committing the first few sentences of your introduction to memory will help you "get on" well with your presentation and feel more secure under pressure when you start to speak.

- **Check support materials.** Arrange your notes or visual aids before you begin. Adjust the microphone.

- **Stand comfortably.** Position yourself at the podium or square up to the audience. Set your feet so you are comfortably balanced.

- **Get set before you speak.** Take a moment to relax your neck and shoulders. Focus your thoughts and your energy.

- **Remember to breathe.** Take a deep breath to settle yourself, and let it out slowly.

- **Look at the audience.** Make eye contact before you say anything. Find a friendly face in the audience to help you feel more at ease.

- **Greet the audience.** A warm, friendly greeting before you begin the introduction can help you connect with the audience. Say hello to people you know; thank those who invited you; say how happy you are to be there.

- **Show enthusiasm.** Deliver the first few sentences of your introduction (the ones you memorized) with gusto. Make a dynamic first impression.

- **Use your body.** Plan to use a big gesture immediately. Reach out to the audience. Smile!

- **Don't play for sympathy.** Never admit you feel nervous or unprepared. Put the audience at ease.

- **Don't denigrate yourself or your topic.** Never suggest that your presentation is going to be uninteresting, irrelevant, or difficult to follow.

GUIDELINES FOR EFFECTIVE CONCLUSIONS

The second most complex part of a speech, after the introduction, is the conclusion. Most inexperienced speakers have a tendency to finish a speech with an empty comment, like "That's about it." They waste an opportunity to inspire the audience with upbeat, thought-provoking concluding remarks that will drive home their message. Like a good introduction, an effective conclusion has three important functions to fulfill in a short time. Ideally these functions mirror in reverse order the functions of an effective introduction. A good conclusion should wrap up the speech, reinforce the speaker's interest and commitment, and leave a lasting impression.

Wrapping up the Speech

There is a common misconception that in the conclusion the speaker is supposed to summarize the main points in the speech. But a conclusion that simply repeats what has already been covered is typically uninteresting and uninspiring. A good conclusion can do much more than summarize. Think of the conclusion as a time to "wrap up" the topic in a way that complements how you introduced it. Although wrapping up a speech may include summarizing its main points, this summary should bring the audience to a new level of understanding about the topic, not simply restate the main points or arguments. If you have done a thorough job presenting information and evidence in the body of the speech, the audience will want you to tie everything together at the end, to reveal the "the bottom line" about your topic. Notice, for example, how the speaker incorporates summary in this conclusion for a persuasive speech advocating corporate day care:

> *Finally, instituting corporate day care is a decision no one will regret. Imagine how satisfying it will be for working parents at this company to feel secure about the care their children receive, going to work knowing their children are nearby and well cared for. This feeling of satisfaction can only increase company loyalty and productivity. Every company that has instituted corporate day care reports a decrease in absenteeism and an increase in applications. Though in-house day care may seem a large initial investment, in the long run it will be cheaper, in both work-hours and productivity, than no day care. It is an investment in the future—the future of the company and the future of the country.*

We see that the speaker is clearly summarizing some of the main points from the body of her speech in the conclusion: employee satisfaction, increased loyalty and productivity, success at other companies. But all of these arguments are leading up to the bottom-line position that day care is "an investment in the future." This phrase ties together all the speaker's arguments and wraps up her appeal for child day-care service at her company.

One of the best ways to wrap up a speech is to return to an interesting anecdote or example presented in the introduction, to bring the presentation back full circle to where it began. Naturally, you should not simply *repeat* the opening story, but you should try to bring out new, salient meanings or nuances in it. Remember, you want to bring the audience to a higher understanding and appreciation of your topic, not simply rehash what you already said.

For example, how would you advise Jason to conclude his speech about the dangers of lawn tractors? How might he use the story of his mower accident as a reprise in the conclusion to wrap up his presentation?

Reinforcing the Speaker's Interest and Commitment

The second important function of an effective conclusion is to reinforce the speaker's interest in and commitment to the topic, which complements the introduction's function to establish the speaker's credibility. The conclusion is your last chance to convey to the audience your passion and concern for your topic. One way to do this is to include the audience in your cause by employing the first-person plural pronouns "we" and "us," especially in a *call to action* at the end of the speech. For example: "The use of chlordane must be stopped! And the responsibility lies with *us*. *We* must take the steps that can prevent *our* families, *our* friends and *ourselves* from the harmful effects of chlordane poisoning."

Another way to reinforce your interest and commitment in the conclusion is to endorse your topic personally, as in this call to action in a speech about eye surgery: "Lasik eye surgery changed my life. So if you also want to correct your vision so you don't have to wear corrective lenses, then I urge you to consider it. I believe it will change your life too!"

Most important, you should reinforce your interest and commitment by demonstrating energy and enthusiasm for the topic when you deliver the conclusion. For example, imagine how you might deliver this concluding comment for a speech about drug testing:

> *I urge all of you, whether you are guilty or not, to resist the irrational*
> *use of drug tests in the workplace in order to protect your privacy.*
> *Refusing a drug test could possibly cost you your job. But complying*
> *with a drug test will without a doubt cost you your privacy.*

Remember, it will be difficult to convince the audience to share your passion for a topic if you don't show some yourself.

Leaving a Lasting Impression

The final function of a good conclusion, mirroring the need to get the audience's attention in the introduction, is to leave a lasting impression. In fact, you can use any of the attention-getting devices outlined earlier for introductions to create a memorable conclusion for your speech. Some speakers like to use a dramatic statement or quotation as a concluding remark. Others prefer to ask a question that will keep the audience thinking about the topic. Whatever you decide to use for your concluding remarks should be something that will stick with listeners long after you leave the podium. Don't be afraid to take a few risks to make a lasting impression with the conclusion. Make it dramatic or humorous, personal or cosmic, but make it memorable.

If you think of the introduction and conclusion as "bookends" for your presentation and remember that their functions complement one another, you will improve the organization of your speech, making it more unified and coherent. Think of the introduction and conclusion as a pair of mini-speeches that mirror each other. Plan and prepare them separately from the rest of the speech. Rehearse them separately as well until you feel secure and confident about delivering them.

TIPS FOR DELIVERING THE CONCLUSION

Because the conclusion of your speech is the last impression the audience has of you, you want it to be a strong impression. Here are some tips to help you deliver the conclusion to best advantage:

- **Indicate that you are ready to conclude.** Set the conclusion apart from the body of the speech with a pause and/or a change of body position. This is a good opportunity to move closer to the audience.
- **Make eye contact before you conclude.** Look for listeners who have been most interested and attentive to your presentation.
- **Provide a transition to the conclusion.** "In conclusion" or "finally" are signals to the audience that you are wrapping up the presentation.
- **Don't drag out the conclusion.** The audience may lose patience if you announce "in conclusion" but continue to drone on.
- **Incorporate pauses in the conclusion.** Dramatic pauses can be very effective for creating a lasting impression. Don't rush your concluding remarks.
- **Don't let the conclusion undermine your credibility.** Never suggest, either verbally or nonverbally, that the presentation has been difficult or unpleasant for you.
- **Maintain confidence and control to the very end.** Be careful not to lapse into nervous behaviors. Don't give up on your speech and throw in the towel.
- **Deliver closing remarks with emphasis.** Finish your speech with energy and enthusiasm. Don't conclude with, "That's about it."
- **After the conclusion, pause before you sit down or take questions.** If the audience applauds, acknowledge it. Don't start walking to your seat while you are still speaking.

 **CONCLUSION**

Most experienced speakers and speech coaches acknowledge that introductions and conclusions are two of the most challenging components of a presentation to prepare and deliver effectively. But they also acknowledge that the introduction and conclusion are golden opportunities to create a memorable impression for you and your message. Good introductions and conclusions can have a powerful impact on the audience. They are what the audience is most likely to remember from your speech. So as you prepare your presentation, keep in mind the old Vaudeville axiom, "Know how to get on, know how to get off, and the rest will take care of itself."

Building Basic
Presentation Skills

"Learning fundamental delivery techniques allows the 'real you'
to emerge when speaking."

When Chris finished his speech on household fire safety, he felt elated because he covered all his major points and did not forget anything. He even remembered the insurance company statistics he wanted to include. On paper, it was a good speech, well-organized and convincing. But when Chris looked at the video of his presentation, he was despondent. He thought, "I prepared so well. What went wrong?" He had researched and organized his speech and outlined it carefully. He had practiced it four times. He had even included reminders in his notes to smile and use pauses.

As Chris watched his video, he saw that technically he had succeeded in presenting all his ideas, but he was shocked at the way he looked and sounded. His body language obviously communicated that he was not comfortable in front of the group. He continually shifted his weight from side to side, especially at the beginning and end of the speech. His hands were clasped in front of his body, his notes hanging loosely in one hand while the other hand grasped the opposite wrist in a death grip. The few hand gestures he used near the end of the speech looked timid and ineffectual. His head was down most of the time, and he made only brief, fleeting eye contact with the audience during the speech. He felt even worse when he had to turn the volume up to the max to hear himself. The final blow was that he counted twenty-seven "ums" and "ahs" in his short speech. How could so many things go wrong with a speech that was so solid on paper?

Watching his video, Chris faced a harsh moment of truth that many beginning speakers experience. His shyness and anxiety about speaking in front of a group caused him to react in ways he had not expected. He was not even conscious of these reactions as he was presenting his speech, yet they prevented him from delivering his thoughtful, well-organized message effectively. In fact, they prevented him from even "being himself" in front of the audience.

The lesson Chris learned from watching his video is that good content is not enough to make a good speech. Research shows that 70 to 80 percent of communication is nonverbal. Chris's failure to carry himself with confidence, to project his voice, to make eye contact with the audience, and to use his hands and body effectively all hampered his presentation. Speakers who do not employ these physical, nonverbal components of public speaking effectively are limiting themselves severely.

This chapter covers the basic presentation skills necessary to look good, sound good, and connect with the audience when you deliver a speech. By understanding and practicing the physical components of public speaking, you can greatly enhance your presentation style and allow the real you, the natural you, to speak confidently before the audience.

LOOKING GOOD

Public speaking is not only an intellectual activity, but also a physical activity. Like any other physical activity in our lives, such as driving a car or hitting a tennis ball, it is possible to get better at public speaking by learning a few basic skills. If you want to look and feel your best when you give a speech, there are a few fundamentals that you need to learn and employ. The following are some best practices for looking good when you give a speech.

Dress for Success

The audience forms an impression of you even before you begin to speak. Appearance is important. You should carefully consider what you will wear for your presentation. Select clothes that are appropriate for the speaking occasion and that will also make you look good, feel comfortable, and be yourself.

Part of audience analysis is to determine what the expected "dress code" is for your audience. But even for the most formal speaking situations you should choose clothing within the dress code range that will flatter your appearance and help you feel good about yourself. When in doubt, overdress a little. You can always take off your jacket or dressy scarf if the situation is more informal than you expected. For classroom presentations, choose clothing that will not detract from your message. Your choice of clothes sends a message to the audience that your presentation is important, that you take it seriously, and that they should as well.

Project a Confident Image

Your presentation begins not with your first words, but with the first glimpse the audience has of you. Therefore, it is important to create a good first impression. Even if you are feeling nervous, try to project confidence. When it is time for your presentation, collect yourself and move confidently to where you will speak. Keep your head up, glance at individuals in the audience, and smile if it is appropriate. Take your time. Be sure you feel settled and completely ready before you begin to speak. Take a moment to check that your notes are in order and the microphone is positioned correctly. Take a deep breath, let it out slowly, and remind yourself to project confidence throughout the speech. Remember the conventional wisdom from competitive sports: "If you don't show confidence, your opponent already has the advantage." In public speaking the opponent is your anxiety monster, the shy and anxious part of yourself that will try to sabotage your carefully prepared message, as it did for Chris, unless you project confidence to keep it in check.

Set Your Feet

Many speakers betray their nervousness with their feet. Shifting weight and swaying from side to side, as Chris did in his presentation, rocking on heels, shuffling or tapping the feet, standing awkwardly with one foot crossed behind the other, or leaning away from the audience with weight on the back foot are all indications that the speaker does not feel grounded and settled. Like hitting a good tennis or golf shot, public speaking starts with a good "stance." In physical activities like these, if your stance is not comfortable and balanced, your body cannot feel relaxed and responsive. Before you begin to speak, find a stance that feels comfortable to you. Most people look and feel comfortable if they set their feet about shoulder-width apart with their weight balanced evenly on both feet. Women sometimes prefer to stand with the heel of one foot angled against the other instep, especially for more formal speaking situations, but a more open stance is also perfectly acceptable. You should position yourself so you can see everyone in the audience without having to move or turn your body. This is called *squaring up* to the audience. If you are using visual aids for your presentation, square up so you will be able to see both the visual aid and the audience comfortably.

Once you set your feet, you don't need to think about your stance again, unless you move to another spot. If you do move, make it purposeful movement, and be sure to set your feet again. Purposeful movement—to get closer to the audience, to emphasize a point, to indicate a transition in your speech, to answer a question, or to interact with your visual aids—can make your presentation more animated and dynamic. But too much movement, or random movement, will look like nervous activity and become a distraction for the audience. On a *Business Week* website Carmine Gallo, a communications coach who works with business professionals, identifies "The 10 Worst Presentation Habits." One of the bad habits on his list is "fidgeting, jiggling, and swaying," all of which reflect nervousness or insecurity that stem from not feeling grounded. Good communicators make every effort to eliminate annoying movement and mannerisms when they present and to maintain good posture and body control. This all begins with setting your feet when you speak.

Engage Your Hands

Whereas moving your feet can make you look nervous and uneasy, moving your upper body usually makes you look confident and energetic. All of us to some extent speak with our hands in normal conversation. Moving our hands when we speak is part of how we express ourselves, complementing and emphasizing our words. You will look much better if you become comfortable using your hands for public speaking as well. You can actually handicap your presentation if you try to speak without using your hands or if you restrict them somehow so they don't move naturally and expressively.

Because many speakers feel self-conscious about their hands in front of an audience, they often try, either consciously or unconsciously, to hide or immobilize their hands. They adopt postures that inhibit or eliminate the natural expressiveness of hand gestures. Speech coaches sometimes create nicknames for these postures:

- *fig leaf*—hands clasped together in front of the body below the belt
- *reverse fig leaf*—hands clasped together behind the back
- *broken wrist*—one hand with a death grip on the opposite wrist
- *hobo*—both hands in trouser or jacket pockets
- *bouncer*—arms folded and locked over the chest
- *parson*—hands folded or steepled as in prayer
- *drill instructor* (or *cheerleader*)—both hands on hips
- *little tea pot*—one hand on the hip

In addition, there are many nervous behaviors or activities that can advertise a speaker's uneasiness, such as fiddling with notes or eye glasses, twirling hair or pulling at a mustache, scratching an earlobe, and jingling loose change in pockets. These nervous activities, called *adapters*, can distract (and sometimes annoy) the audience and make the speaker look awkward, unsure, or uncomfortable.

There are three simple solutions for these problems with awkward use of hands and distracting adapters:

- **Keep your hands above your waist.** When you speak to someone from a seated position, from an easy chair or at a desk for example, where are your hands? Most likely they are bent at the elbows and moving freely in front of your upper body. So when you speak in a standing position, why would you let your hands hang at your sides? Hand gestures below the waist look small and ineffectual; they look like penguin flippers. When you begin to speak, remind yourself to keep your hands above your waist, where they will look more natural and expressive than at your sides.

- **Keep your hands open.** In all the postures listed above the speaker's hands cannot gesture naturally or expressively because they are locked together. If you find yourself in these postures, you have effectively "handcuffed" yourself and eliminated hand gestures from your speech. But if you keep your hands open, they will move and gesture freely on their own. You do not have to think about them. If you are speaking with notes, hold them in one hand, leaving the other hand free to gesture. Try not to gesture with the notes. For informal presentations it is acceptable to keep one hand in your pocket, but be sure to gesture generously with the other hand.

FIGURE 4.1
Keep hands "up and open" to look more relaxed and confident when
presenting.

- **Use a broad gesture in your opening remarks.** Engaging your hands energetically
  at the beginning of your speech helps you loosen up, overcome early jitters and
  nervous energy, and look more confident and enthusiastic. It also encourages you to
  gesture more freely through rest of the presentation.

During your presentation if you drop your hands or find them "handcuffed" in any way,
unlock them immediately and bring them to the "up and open" position. Remember, you
are not communicating to full capacity if you do not engage your hands.

Use Facial Expression

We also communicate with facial expressions. In most situations, facial expressions convey
emotions, moods, and attitudes far more directly and efficiently than words. Just as you
don't have to think about hand gestures, if you allow your hands to be responsive, you also
do not have to think about facial expressions if you allow yourself to be responsive to the
audience and to your own emotions. If you look at the audience and feel friendly, your face
will relax and smile. If your message is somber or dramatic, your face will express the se-
riousness you feel. If you are passionate about your topic, your face will show enthusiasm.

Remember that the audience sees your facial expression before they hear your words. Thus you have the power to set the mood and tone of your presentation even before you begin your opening remarks. When you are ready to address the audience, focus on the feelings you want to communicate and just let them come through. As with hand gestures, it is good to put more energy into facial expression at the beginning of the speech to help you loosen up and channel your energy. Most of the time, a friendly smile will work just fine. During the presentation let your feelings match your words, and your facial expressions will match your message.

USE NOTES EFFECTIVELY

At the very top of the list of "The 10 Worst Presentation Habits" cited in *Business Week* is "reading from notes." Nothing breaks the rapport between listener and audience more quickly than a presenter reading directly from a script, notes, or PowerPoint slides.

The best advice about using notes is don't use them if another visual aid can do the job better. Because in the back of your mind you know that the audience cannot see your notes, you may be tempted to write down too much, thinking that more information will make your presentation easier. Then, during your speech you suddenly realize that you cannot read your notes because the writing is too small, illegible, or poorly blocked out. All the facts and figures you crammed into your notes with a fine number 3 pencil are completely washed out under the florescent lights in the room. Consequently, the notes you were counting on to help you have become your enemy instead.

If you must use notes for your presentation, use note cards and follow these tips for using them effectively, so your notes will work *for* you, not *against* you:

- **Use as few cards as possible.** The fewer cards you need to handle, the less likely you will get into trouble by mishandling them. The speaker's ultimate nightmare is to fumble with a stack of cards and scatter them all over the floor. Try to put all the main points of your presentation on one 5 × 7 inch note card. If you have a lot of quotes, add additional cards, but sparingly, and number them.

- **Use as few words as possible.** Most people try to put too much information on note cards, which almost always creates problems. Except for direct quotes, there is no reason to write out complete sentences on note cards. Instead, identify key words and phrases (such as proper names, key terms, important dates or statistics, catchy expressions, etc.) that can serve as *prompts* for your main talking points. You can distill a great deal of information into a few key words. For example, as you can see from the sample note card in figure 4.2 for a presentation on "Tips for Using Note Cards," you can condense this entire paragraph down to "Use few words." Limiting the words on the note card will also help guard against the biggest pitfall: *reading* your ideas from the note card instead of *presenting* them.

Tips for Using Note Cards

▼ **Use 1 card**

▼ **Use few words**

▼ **Write 1 side only**

▼ **Print BIG notes**

▼ **Hold in 1 hand**
   Keep card steady
   Gestures!

▼ **Look at Audience**

*Remember to Breathe

FIGURE 4.2

- **Write only on one side of the note card.** This will eliminate possible confusion or mishandling from having to flip cards over as you speak. Also, if you use more than one card, be sure to number them clearly and check that they are in correct order before you speak. And you can add short remainders, such as "Remember to Breathe"
- **Write notes legibly.** Write, or better yet *print*, in large, clear lettering that you will be able to see and read easily. Don't use a light pencil, but rather a dark felt-tip pen, and be sure to leave enough white space on the card so you can pick out each note at a glance. You can also use color highlighters to emphasize the most important headings or notes.
- **Hold note cards in one hand when you present.** A common problem of presenting with note cards is that speakers sometimes "handcuff" themselves by holding them with both hands. You can prevent this problem by holding note cards in one hand and allowing the other hand to gesture freely. Remember to keep both hands above the waist. Avoid gesturing with the note card since this can become an annoying distraction. You may switch note cards to the other hand, if you wish, just so one hand is always free to gesture.
- **Pause to look at note cards.** The biggest trap speakers fall into when presenting with note cards is reading directly from them, thus undermining effective eye contact with the audience. Except for brief glances to your note card when reading a direct quote, look at people in the audience, not at your note cards, whenever you are speaking. If you need to look at your note card, pause and glance down at it long enough to prepare your next talking point. Then look up at the audience and continue speaking. It is not true that the audience will think you are unprepared if you use notes. In fact, if you bring organized notes for the presentation, the audience will perceive this as an indication that you are well prepared. So don't be afraid to pause, take advantage of your notes, and use them confidently.

SOUNDING GOOD

There are also some basic practices and procedures you should follow to sound good when you deliver your presentation.

Project Your Voice

No matter how enlightening or inspiring your message may be, it will be wasted if your audience cannot hear it. Unfortunately, speakers like Chris never even realize that their message is lost on the audience until it is too late. But fortunately Chris learned a valuable lesson from watching his video and realized how to improve his voice projection.

In public speaking, voice projection is not a matter of personal style; it is a survival skill. The bottom line is that if everyone in the room does not hear you clearly, you are not an

effective speaker. If you have a microphone available, you probably don't need to be concerned about voice projection. If you don't have a microphone, it should be your first concern.

The problem for inexperienced speakers like Chris is not that they cannot project their voice; it is that they don't *know* that they need to project more. Experienced speakers notice body language of people in the audience who are having difficulty hearing the speech—for example, listeners leaning toward the speaker, turning their heads, straining to hear. More important, experienced speakers know how to control and adjust the volume of their voice for different speaking situations. Here are a few suggestions to help you project your voice better, with or without a microphone:

- **Speak to the back of the room.** In ordinary conversations we naturally project our voice to reach our listeners, no matter how much distance separates us. You instinctively know how loud to talk to your friend across the kitchen table or across a noisy cafeteria. When you speak before a large group, the best way to be sure your voice is loud enough is to speak to individuals who are farthest from you. If the people in the back of the room can hear you clearly, then so can everyone else in the audience.

- **Compensate for background noise.** Be aware of extraneous noise in the room during your presentation. You may have to increase your volume to compensate for noise from outside traffic, ventilation fans, or paper shuffling. Even "white noise" from a laptop computer may require you to raise your voice a notch.

- **Develop breath control.** Listen to professional singers or stage actors, and notice how they breathe during their performances. You will see how important breath control is for good phrasing and voice projection. Public speakers also need to breathe efficiently to project clearly to the back of the room and to avoid running out of breath in the middle of a sentence. To develop better breath control practice increasing the number of words that you can comfortably say in one breath. If you take shallow breaths after every few words or if your voice trails off at the end of sentences, pause and take in more "air support."

- **Speak in a lower pitch.** Most speakers, women and men alike, project better and sound better if they keep their voice in a lower register. A deep-pitched voice usually carries farther and sounds more relaxed and confident than a high-pitched voice.

- **Enunciate clearly.** Projecting effectively involves more than the volume and pitch of the voice. The audience may also miss your message if they cannot understand your words. Take care to enunciate clearly, especially the endings of words or combinations of words with back-to-back consonants. Broadcast announcers learn to pronounce each "t" distinctly in phrases like "last time" or "neat trick."

Control Your Speaking Pace

To project and enunciate more effectively in presentations most of us need to speak more slowly than we do in normal conversation. Yet nervous energy associated with public speaking tends to make us speak faster than usual. Consequently, for inexperienced speakers one of the most difficult parts of sounding good is settling upon a comfortable speaking pace. Many speakers unconsciously set a speaking pace that is too fast for themselves, as well as for the audience. By rushing their delivery, getting ahead of their thoughts, or stumbling over words, they sound nervous; and that in turn makes the audience feel uneasy.

Chapter 1, "Managing Anxiety about Public Speaking," offers suggestions for setting a comfortable speaking pace. Here they are briefly:

- **Use pauses.** Pauses help you slow down and help the audience absorb your message. Build pauses into the script or the outline of your speech; practice using pauses when you rehearse.

- **Don't rush your opening remarks.** The introduction helps set a comfortable pace for the rest of the speech.

- **Hit the "reset button."** Monitor your speaking rate. If you notice yourself speeding up, take a pause and slow down.

- **Compensate while rehearsing.** If you have tendency to rush, practice speaking even more slowly than you would in the actual presentation.

Vary Your Speaking Patterns

We have all encountered speakers who lose our interest quickly because they speak in a monotone voice or because they use the same vocal inflection over and over. Varying your sentence patterns to sound more natural and spontaneous can also enhance your presentation style. Listening to and imitating accomplished actors, broadcasters, and public figures can teach us a lot about how to make our speaking patterns more interesting. Here are a few tricks the professionals use:

- **Vary your pitch.** Most people have a vocal range of several octaves, but use only a limited part of it when presenting. Try to bring more vocal color and variety to your presentations by using a broader pitch range, as we typically do in animated conversations with friends.

- **Vary your tone.** When preparing your speech, look for opportunities to include various emotional tones. A good speech can be both serious and lighthearted, personal and theoretical, dramatic and understated. Adapt your delivery style to match the emotional tone you want to communicate.

- **Vary your pace.** Once you feel in control of your speaking pace, vary it for interesting effects. Speed up to heighten energy and excitement; slow down for dramatic emphasis. Watch the audience for signs that you may need to move more quickly or slowly through your material.

- **Vary your inflections.** One current popular speech pattern, especially among young people, is to finish every sentence as if it were a question, that is, to lift the sound of the final word rather than drop it as we ordinarily do after a statement. Some language experts call this inflection "up talk" or "the Valley Girl syndrome." Any unvarying inflection can become tedious for the audience after a few minutes. Listen carefully to the videos of your speeches. If your delivery sounds monotonous or repetitive, practice using more varied inflections.

- **Use dramatic pauses.** Although a pause of two or three seconds may seem like interminable "dead air" when you are at the podium, using such a pause at the right moment in a speech for dramatic effect can have a powerful impact on an audience. To use dramatic pauses effectively you need to be in control of your speaking pace and in touch with your audience.

Eliminate Verbal Tics

When Chris watched the video of his speech he was surprised and dismayed to discover that he says "um" and "ah" so often, having counted twenty-seven of them in his short presentation. Like many of us, he was not aware that he uses *vocalized pauses*, as these verbal tics are called, so frequently. Chris is certainly not alone. Even the best speakers occasionally use vocalizers to fill empty spaces in their speeches. Expressions such as "okay," "you know," "like," and "really," used repeatedly, are additional examples of verbal tics that can detract from a presentation.

Using vocalizers is a deeply ingrained habit for most people, one that cannot be eliminated easily. Some people are not even aware that they use them. So if you simply resolve not to say "um" and "ah" in your next speech, you are probably setting yourself up for disappointment and failure. As with any deeply ingrained habit, you need to work consistently on eliminating vocalizers over an extended period of time. Here's an example of how such a strategy might work:

> *Miriam watched the video of her persuasive presentation and
> noticed that she said "you know?" countless times during the
> speech. Until she listened to her speech, Miriam was not even
> aware that she used this phrase so frequently, sometimes as often
> as three times in one sentence. She was dismayed at how she
> looked and sounded on the video. Her presentation on fetal alcohol
> syndrome was a serious persuasive speech, but she thought that
> continually saying "you know?" made her look like an "airhead."
> Miriam's friend Tina offered to help her work on this verbal tic.
> Whenever they talked together, over lunch or a cup of coffee or
> even chatting on the telephone, Tina would say "Yes, I know"
> every time Miriam said "you know?" At first Miriam found Tina's
> response annoying because it disrupted the flow of their
> conversation. But Tina was persistent, and eventually Miriam
> learned to anticipate when she was about to say "you know?"
> and to pause instead.*

The technique that Tina used to help Miriam eliminate "you know?" from her speech is a good model for the kind of behavioral training you can use to reinforce or eliminate specific behaviors when you speak. Deeply ingrained habits, such as beginning every new thought with "um," "ah," or "you know," cannot be changed overnight; they must be "deactivated" gradually. The strategy Tina used to help Miriam involved four separate steps. To change an undesirable behavior you need to:

1. ***Identify* the behavior you want to change.** Be as specific as possible. Miriam's goal is not *to improve her speaking style,* but specifically *to eliminate "you know."*

2. ***Monitor* the behavior.** This means you have to become aware of when the behavior occurs. Part of Miriam's problem is that she doesn't even hear herself say "you know," not only in presentations but also in ordinary conversations. Tina serves as a monitor for Miriam, helping her friend become aware of the distracting habit. To monitor this behavior on her own Miriam would need to hear herself saying "you know."

3. ***Anticipate* the behavior.** The next step is for Miriam to anticipate when she is about to say "you know," that is, to be aware of the vocalized pause *before* she actually uses it.

4. *Substitute* **a desirable behavior.** The final step is for Miriam to eliminate the distracting habit and substitute a desirable behavior, in this case to use a pause instead of "you know."

This monitoring process can also help reinforce desirable habits. Let's say, for example, that you sound better when using your voice in a lower register. But when you feel nervous, your voice tends to range higher and sound a bit squeaky. On the video you notice that when your voice is in the right range you speak more slowly; but when your voice is high, you are rushing. Once you understand the interconnection between these sets of behaviors, you can use them to reinforce the activity you want. So, when you hear your voice getting higher, you slow down. When you start feeling rushed, you lower your voice.

 # CONNECTING WITH THE AUDIENCE

It is possible to look good and sound good when you deliver your speech and still be an ineffective speaker if you do not connect with the audience, which is the third set of basic presentation skills. The following are three important best practices to follow in order to connect with the audience

Make Eye Contact

Another bad habit high on *BusinessWeek*'s list of "The 10 Worst Presentation Habits" is "avoiding eye contact." As the website points out, effective public speakers "understand that eye contact is critical to building trust, credibility, and rapport" with the audience. Therefore, if Chris had to pick only one weakness to work on following his unsuccessful speech on household fire safely, it should be his lack of eye contact. Inexperienced speakers frequently undervalue the importance of eye contact in their presentations. Some students even believe in the myth that it is better to look at a spot on the back wall than to look directly at people in the audience. But eye contact is probably the most important nonverbal communication skill for effective public speaking. Eye contact enables a speaker to engage the audience and to receive feedback from them at the same time. Good eye contact is usually what distinguishes speakers who "talk at" the audience and those who "talk with" the audience. Effective eye contact, sometimes described as "listening to the audience with your eyes," is one of the best tools for making a speech a two-way communication.

Good public speakers, even if they are working with notes or visual aids, make eye contact with individuals in the audience at least 80 to 90 percent of the time that they are speaking. The best speakers make eye contact virtually every moment that they are in front of the audience. Here are five suggestions that can help you be more effective at making eye contact with your audience:

- **Look at interested individuals.** This is a good way to break the ice at the beginning of a presentation. Pick out people in the audience who are tuned in to you, and speak to them. Gradually expand your pool of attentive listeners until you feel comfortable making eye contact with everyone in the group.

- **Give a little piece of your speech to each individual.** It is much less intimidating to think of your speech as a series of one-on-one conversations than as an address to a large, impersonal group. So deliver a little bit of your speech to each attentive listener, as if you were conversing casually with each one.

- **Maintain eye contact for three to five seconds.** To some speakers who are not comfortable making eye contact, this may seem like a long time to be looking at a person. But three to five seconds is about the right amount of time to make listeners feel you are paying attention to them but not staring at them. After some practice, you will get into a rhythm and be able to feel when to move your eye contact to the next person. If people in the audience break off eye contact with you first, it may indicate that you are looking at them too long.

- **Try to make eye contact with everyone in the audience.** To connect with the audience as completely as possible you should try to make every person in the audience feel included in your presentation. If you try to make people feel at ease and if you are persistent in your efforts to make eye contact, eventually even the more reticent people will reciprocate your interest.

- **Be especially careful to maintain eye contact when you work with visual aids.** Using notes, props, flip charts, PowerPoint slides, or other visual aids can be a tremendous asset for any presentation. But visual aids can also draw your attention away from the audience. (See Chapter 5 for suggestions on how to use visual aids effectively.)

Involve the Audience

Another way to connect with the audience is to get them involved, either physically or psychologically, in your presentation. Just as a good teacher gets a class of students involved with a lesson, a good speaker gets the audience involved with his or her topic. Here are some simple ways to get the audience involved with your speech:

- **Ask a question.** If you get people in the audience to raise their hands or nod their heads, you've elicited a reaction that involves them physically with your presentation. If you make them think about your question, you've gotten them psychologically involved. Don't underestimate the importance of these small actions. Telemarketers, for instance, know that if they can keep a customer on the phone long enough to answer a few questions, they have a better chance of making a sale. So, pose a question that will help keep the audience on the line with you.

- **Invite questions or comments.** If you tell the audience that you would welcome questions and comments during or after the presentation, they will be thinking about questions they might want to ask you. Some people may even take notes.

- **Compliment the audience.** People always like to hear good things about themselves or their organization. Honor your audience by mentioning some quality that you admire about them. Let them know that you are pleased they invited you to address them. Praise them for their accomplishments, their service, or their dedication.

- **Relate your topic to the audience's experience.** Part of your audience analysis should be to gather specific information about them that you can incorporate into your presentation. Use the names of individuals in the group, refer to past or current achievements, include examples related to their experience, or mention how your topic addresses their needs. Show the audience that you are taking an interest in them.

- **Give the audience a simple task.** Ask them to write a short list, to express a preference, to examine an object, to solve a riddle, to recall a past event—almost anything that will convert people in the audience from passive observers into active participants. There used to be a clichéd college orientation speech for new students that began: "Take a good look at the person on your left and at the person on your right. A year from now, one of them will be gone." This simple activity would usually pique the interest of at least half the people in the audience.

Use the Audience's Energy

One other thing you can do to connect with the audience is to tap into the interest and enthusiasm listeners have for your topic. Anyone who has some theater experience knows how much energy a lively audience can generate for the performance. There are some people in any audience who are eager to listen and learn. You can recognize them immediately by their interested body language—upright in their seats, leaning toward you, making eye contact, smiling or nodding at your opening remarks. Zero in on these people, soak up their interest and enthusiasm, and reflect it back to others in the audience. These engaged listeners make you feel better about yourself and your message, more confident and secure, and more willing to put yourself out for the audience. This kind of positive energy can be contagious. You can tap into it and use it to make yourself a more engaging and dynamic speaker. Sometimes people who have avoided public speaking all their lives get hooked on it after they experience an exciting exchange of energy with a lively audience. It is a satisfying feeling for speech teachers and coaches to watch their students and clients experience this energy and excitement for the first time.

 # CONCLUSION

This chapter has discussed basic presentation skills that can help you look good, sound good, and connect with the audience when you deliver your speech. These are physical skills that, with practice, you can develop and eventually master. Don't be discouraged if you don't get immediate results. After all, you won't learn to play the guitar or drive a golf ball overnight either. But if you work at these skills, you will become a more competent and confident public speaker.

One of the keys to developing better presentation skills is to recognize that looking good, sounding good, and connecting with the audience are all closely interrelated. None of these skills functions in isolation. Quite often a speaker can solve several presentation problems by changing one behavior. Chris, for example, neither looked good nor sounded good in his fire safety speech because he kept his head down and did not project his voice. But he could change both of these undesirable behaviors with one adjustment, by simply making good eye contact with individuals at the back of the audience. Some students discover, for instance, that when they begin to use their hands more naturally, their speaking pace slows down, they say fewer "ums" and "ahs," and they pay closer attention to the audience.

With practice you can also discover how your speaking behaviors are interrelated. When you rehearse your speeches and review your videos, watch how all the basic components of good presentation—feet, hands, voice, and eyes—affect one another. There is no magic pill that will turn you into a dynamic speaker overnight, but thoughtful analysis of your delivery style and determination to improve it may lead to insights that will catapult you toward becoming the poised and confident public speaker you want to be.

TIPS AT A GLANCE FOR IMPROVING BASIC PRESENTATION SKILLS

Looking Good

- Dress for success.
- Project a confident image.
- Set your feet comfortably.
- Keep your hands up and open.
- Use facial expression.
- Use notes effectively

Sounding Good

- Project your voice.
- Control your speaking pace.
- Vary your speaking patterns.
- Eliminate verbal tics.

Connecting with the Audience

- Make eye contact.
- Involve the audience.
- Use the audience's energy.

CHAPTER 5

Preparing and Using
Visual Aids

*"Visual aids are supportive friends that help
strengthen communication with your audience."*

Michelle had been out of high school for nearly twenty years, raising three children on a horse farm in rural New Jersey. When she came back to college, she lacked self-confidence and worried that she would not be able to keep up academically. She thought that taking a public speaking course would help reconnect her with the academic world. But when she got up to introduce herself in class at the beginning of the semester, she stood with her head down, looking at the floor, her hands locked behind her back, and struggled to say a few barely audible sentences. It was a painful experience for her, as well as for the rest of the class. She looked as if she were about to be executed. No one in the class that day would have guessed that at the end of the semester Michelle would deliver an animated, insightful ten-minute presentation entitled "Life on the Backstretch" based on her experience handling horses behind the scenes at a race track. (See Figure 5.1.) Her speech drew an enthusiastic response from the audience and earned her an A+ grade.

"I was a basket case at the beginning of the semester," Michelle admits. "I was terrified that I would forget everything I wanted to say when I got up to speak the first time. And I did!" So what was the key to Michelle's dramatic transformation into a dynamic, confident speaker in just a few weeks? The answer is that she developed a strategy to overcome the fear that she would forget her speech. And the linchpin in her strategy was to use visual aids for her speeches.

71

Life on the Backstretch

Behind the Scenes at the Racetrack

FIGURE 5.1

"Things started to turn around for me," Michelle recalls, "when I realized how much structure visual aids could give my speeches and help me remember what I wanted to say." Michelle learned that a small investment of time and effort to prepare visual aids before a speech can yield huge dividends when it is time to deliver it. She was also pleasantly surprised to learn from her evaluations that her classmates thought the visuals made her presentation more interesting, and easier to follow and remember.

This chapter explains why you should use visual aids and offers practical suggestions for how to prepare and use them effectively. (Note: The chapter focuses on visual aids, rather than audio/visual aids. Nevertheless, the abbreviated "A/V" is how public speakers often refer to any kind of aids used to support presentations.)

WHY USE VISUAL AIDS?

A visual aid is any physical object, graphic, or written image that is used to enhance or supplement a speaker's message by allowing the audience to see some aspect of the presentation in addition to hearing it. Visual aids provide many benefits both for audiences and for speakers.

How Visual Aids Benefit the Audience

Here are some ways that visual aids benefit the audience:

- **They help the audience get interested.** One reason Michelle's speech succeeded so well is that her visuals included interesting pictures of people and activities behind the scenes at a racetrack. For people who are unfamiliar with the "backstretch" culture at the track, these images can be fascinating and a sure-fire way to arouse interest.

- **They help the audience absorb new or unfamiliar information.** Michelle added local color to her presentation with racetrack expressions that may not be familiar to a general audience, for example, terms for different classes of race horses, such as "kings" and "queens," "condition" horses, and "claimers." (See Figure 5.2.) Michelle helped the audience understand these specialized terms by incorporating them into her visual aids.

- **They help the audience follow complex events, procedures, or arguments.** There are many complicated activities going on at the track between races. Michelle helped the audience see how they are interrelated by diagramming them on her visuals.

- **They help the audience remember the presentation.** Many studies show that listeners retain verbal information better, in some cases four to five times better, if they also receive visual reinforcement of the information. For example, one study

The Horses

- **Yearlings**
- **Kings and Queens**
- **Conditions**
- **Claimers**
- **Retirement**

FIGURE 5.2

recorded how well listeners can recall information presented verbally and visually after three hours, and after three days:

Presentation	Recall After Three Hours	Recall After Three Days
Verbal only	70 percent	10 percent
Visual only	72 percent	20 percent
Verbal and visual combined	85 percent	65 percent

Those of us at Michelle's presentation will remember most of what we learned about life on the backstretch because she reinforced the information with interesting visual aids and amusing anecdotes. When Michelle finished her presentation, the audience could see what life on the backstretch is actually like.

How Visual Aids Benefit the Speaker

Visual aids can also be a big help to the speaker at every phase of planning, rehearsing, and presenting a speech. Here are some ways visual aids can benefit you as the presenter:

- **They help the speaker establish credibility.** The audience starts to form an opinion of you even before you begin speaking, from your appearance, your posture, and your demeanor. If they see that you have prepared visual aids for your presentation and that you are confident and knowledgeable about how to use them, you will make a good first impression, suggesting that you are well prepared and that your message is important.

- **They help the speaker organize the speech.** Like Michelle, you may find that visual aids greatly help you organize and structure your presentation. In fact, planning the headings and the main points for your A/V right away is an effective strategy for generating and organizing material for a speech.

- **They help the speaker illustrate the speech.** Anyone who has worked on a school newspaper or yearbook, or has tried to produce a business brochure, or website, understands how important visual appearance is to communicating a message to a target audience. Your speech may have greater impact on the audience if your visual aids include images—such as drawings, pictures, graphs, or charts—to illustrate and reinforce your message. Graphics offer an opportunity to bring creativity or personality into a speech. You don't have to be a commercial artist to create visually interesting A/V. Just try to arrange words and images on the page so the eye will be able to see and read them comfortably. Also try to include color, at least on the title page.

- **They help the speaker remember the speech.** From the speaker's perspective, this is perhaps the greatest advantage to using visual aids. For Michelle this was the key to overcoming her communication anxiety. If the main points of your presentation are outlined on visual aids, you cannot "draw a blank" and forget your speech. You may lose incidental bits of information, which sometimes happens even to the best speakers, but you cannot lose the main points or the overall structure of the speech because they are laid out right there on the visuals. All you have to do is turn your head to read them.

- **They help the speaker gain confidence.** Knowing that with visual aids you cannot forget the essential components of your speech can be a tremendous confidence-builder. You will feel more confident at every stage of planning and delivering your speech because you know the visual aids are there to assist you. You have Michelle's assurance on this point, and the assurance of countless others who have learned to become confident public speakers by relying on visual aids.

- **They help the speaker manage anxiety.** This point goes hand in hand with the previous point. If you feel more confident about giving your speech, you will be better able to manage communication anxiety. If the content of your presentation is safely outlined on visual aids, you can concentrate your energy on delivering your speech, not remembering it. Part of your mind will be free to focus on good posture, breathing, speaking pace, eye contact, and other presentation skills that help you look and feel more relaxed.

- **They help the speaker channel energy.** Since presenting with visual aids involves physical activity, they offer an opportunity to put excess nervous energy to good use. Visual aids allow you to use your arms more freely, incorporate "big gestures" into the presentation, and make upper-body movement look more natural.

 # TYPES OF VISUAL AIDS

Depending on the particular circumstances of your presentation, various visual aids are available to you. Even though PowerPoint slides are the most preferred media for visual aids today, both in the academic and the business worlds, a versatile speaker should know how to use several types of visual aids effectively. It is important to find out which A/V media best suit your personality and presentation style and to become proficient with them. Most important of all is to incorporate, if possible, some kind of visual aid in every presentation you make. The following are some types of visual aids you may choose to work with. Later in the chapter there are specific tips for preparing and presenting with visual aids.

Props

Props are physical objects or materials—such as models, tools, athletic equipment, musical instruments, cooking or baking utensils, materials for arts and crafts, and so on—that are included in a presentation to reinforce or illustrate its message. Props usually figure prominently in demonstration speeches where the speaker presents an activity or concept that is not easily explained in words. For example, you would use props if you want to demonstrate how to use a nine iron or administer an insulin injection.

DILBERT: © Scott Adams/Dist. by United Feature Syndicate, Inc.

Flip Charts

A flip chart is a large tablet of paper (about two feet wide by three feet high) that is set on an easel stand so the pages can be "flipped" over the top as the speaker finishes with them. Flip chart pages come either lined or unlined, providing some options for laying out words and images on the pages, either by drawing on them or by attaching images or lettering. Flip charts are a convenient, inexpensive, low-tech visual aid that can be adapted to most speaking situations if the group or the auditorium is not too large. Because they are versatile and dependable, flip charts are often the A/V medium of choice for small business presentations, decision-making meetings, and training sessions. They are also one of the most commonly used visual aids in seminar presentations.

Poster Boards

Poster boards are large sturdy sheets of cardboard on which a speaker can write or attach words and images. The boards may be mounted either on an easel or the wall. Using poster boards as a visual aid is similar to using a flip chart, except that they are more cumbersome to handle if you use more than one board. It is usually more convenient to use a flip chart. The same rules for preparing and presenting with the flip chart apply to poster boards.

Computer Slides

The most preferred medium for visual aids today is computer slides, such as PowerPoint, which offer virtually unlimited possibilities to reinforce and enhance presentations. PowerPoint slides provide tremendous resources for visual aids, such as unlimited background patterns, color combinations, font types and sizes, clip art, digital photographs, video and sound clips, and more. Computer slides are usually projected directly through a computer using an LCD projector, but they can also be printed out as hard-copy handouts. In fact, for important presentations it is good practice to prepare handouts as a back-up for PowerPoint slides, just in case you encounter technical glitches.

Handouts

Handouts are any printed materials that a speaker distributes to the audience as part of a presentation. Handouts are especially useful if a speaker wishes to provide the audience supplementary information or background that will not fit easily on other visual aids. Handouts are also the most practical way to provide back-up for more high-tech A/V, such as PowerPoint presentations.

 # HOW TO USE VISUAL AIDS EFFECTIVELY

From a speaker's perspective the cardinal rule for using visual aids is: Make visual aids your ally for the presentation; never let them become your enemy. After all, they are supposed to be visual *aids*. There are many situations where speakers use visual aids poorly, for example, by presenting a PowerPoint slide with a full typed page of information that no one in the audience can read, or by talking to the flip chart instead of to the audience, or by trying to demonstrate a complicated procedure with props that do not work properly. In such cases ineffective visual aids become an enemy, interfering with the speaker's ability to convey a message and the audience's ability to receive it. They may annoy and alienate an audience, and will almost certainly make the speaker look bad and lose credibility. The following are some suggestions for how to prepare and use various visual aids effectively. These tips can help make visual aids your ally, not your enemy.

Tips for Using Props

- **Make sure the audience can see the props.** No matter how interesting your props are, they will work against you if the audience cannot see them well. Make sure the props are large and detailed enough for everyone to see clearly. When you handle props, hold them or display them so that everyone can understand the point you are making with them. If necessary, step closer to the audience or move around the room so people can get a better look. If you are working with immovable props, such as large models or complex apparatus, display them on a table or desk that is positioned so everyone has a clear view.

- **Rehearse with props.** You cannot be sure that your props will work properly and that you will handle them properly unless you rehearse with them. Sometimes even when you practice, props don't work correctly. But experienced speakers try to work out all the bugs by practicing until they feel comfortable their props. They also try to anticipate problems that might arise with props during a presentation.

- **Look at the audience, not the props.** Look closely at television commercials where a celebrity endorses a product. Notice that the spokesperson displays the product so viewers can see it while looking straight into the camera. Try to work

FIGURE 5.3
Display props so everyone can see them clearly, and maintain eye
contact with the audience.

with your props this way. Ideally, you should maintain continuous eye contact
with the audience throughout the presentation. If your props require close
attention or careful handling and you have to look at them as you speak, you
should look up from time to time and make eye contact, even if you have to
interrupt your demonstration. The longer you break eye contact with the audience,
the harder it is to reestablish it.

Tips for Using Flip Charts

Many of the tips for using flips charts also apply to visual aids in other media, such as chalk
boards, poster boards, and computer slides. The examples used in this section are from visual aids that accompanied a classroom presentation on tattoos, entitled "Tattoos: They're
for Life." (See Figures 5.4 through 5.7.)

- **Be sure the audience can see and read information easily.** This is the most
  important rule for any visual aids that include writing or graphics. Remember, your
  visual aids are counterproductive if the audience cannot see and read them
  comfortably. Therefore, take care that all lettering and images are large enough, dark

enough, and legible enough for everyone in the audience to read. Leave enough white space on the page between lines of information, as well as at the top and bottom, so the eye moves evenly over the page and can quickly distinguish each point. Figure 5.5 is an example of how just four words and one simple image well-spaced on the page can effectively illustrate important considerations about "Picking the Place" for a tattoo on the body.

- **Use headings.** Every page of information should have a heading that identifies and unifies the material on that page within the broader perspective of the presentation topic. Like the topic sentences of paragraphs in an essay, these headings are the backbone of a speech, providing a skeletal structure for talking points and examples to flesh out. Good headings help the speaker organize the speech, and help the audience follow the speech. In the speech about tattoos, for example, the speaker uses parallel headings to unify the speech and give it a smooth flow. By repeating the word "Picking" in each heading, the speaker establishes an underlying theme of the speech (choices one needs to make before getting a tattoo) and provides a mnemonic device to help the audience remember the main points of the speech, especially on the final page (figure 5.7) with a twist on the word in "Picking the Scabs."

- **Keep information simple and clear.** Select key words and phrases for visual aids that succinctly convey each important point you want to make. Eliminate extraneous words. Figure 5.6 is a good example. The speaker simply lists four key words on the page, each followed by a question mark, to suggest that these are important questions to ask about the kind of tattoo to choose. Also avoid outlining cues like Roman numerals, capital letters, or numbers on visuals. Use bullets instead. For bullets in the tattoo speech, the speaker drew simple pictures that visually reinforce the key words on the last two pages of the presentation (figures 5.6 and 5.7).

- **Create parallel bullet points.** Keep all the bullet points under each heading parallel. One way to do this is to use the same grammatical structure for phrasing all the bullets on a page. For example, notice that all the bullet points in figure 5.6 are single-word adjectives followed by a question mark and that all the points in figure 5.7 are verb phrases beginning with "keep." In preparing your speech, if you find one point that does not fit the parallel structure of the page, figure out why. Perhaps you need to revise it, or move it under another heading, or eliminate it completely.

- **Double-check spelling.** It is easy to miss spelling errors on visual aids, especially on flip chart pages where words appear much larger than on a standard written page. Even good spellers sometimes overlook mistakes where letters are transposed in words, for example "form" instead of "from." In the A/V for the tattoo speech oversights on words like "offensive" or "proportioned" (in figure 5.6), or even the word "tattoos" in the title, might easily occur if the speaker does not specifically check spelling. Proofread (or ask a better speller to proofread) your A/V before you do the final lettering, and then proof it again when it is all finished.

FIGURE 5.4

Picking the Place

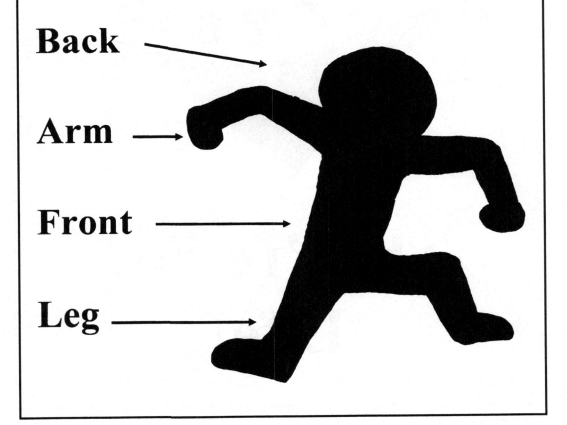

Back

Arm

Front

Leg

FIGURE 5.5

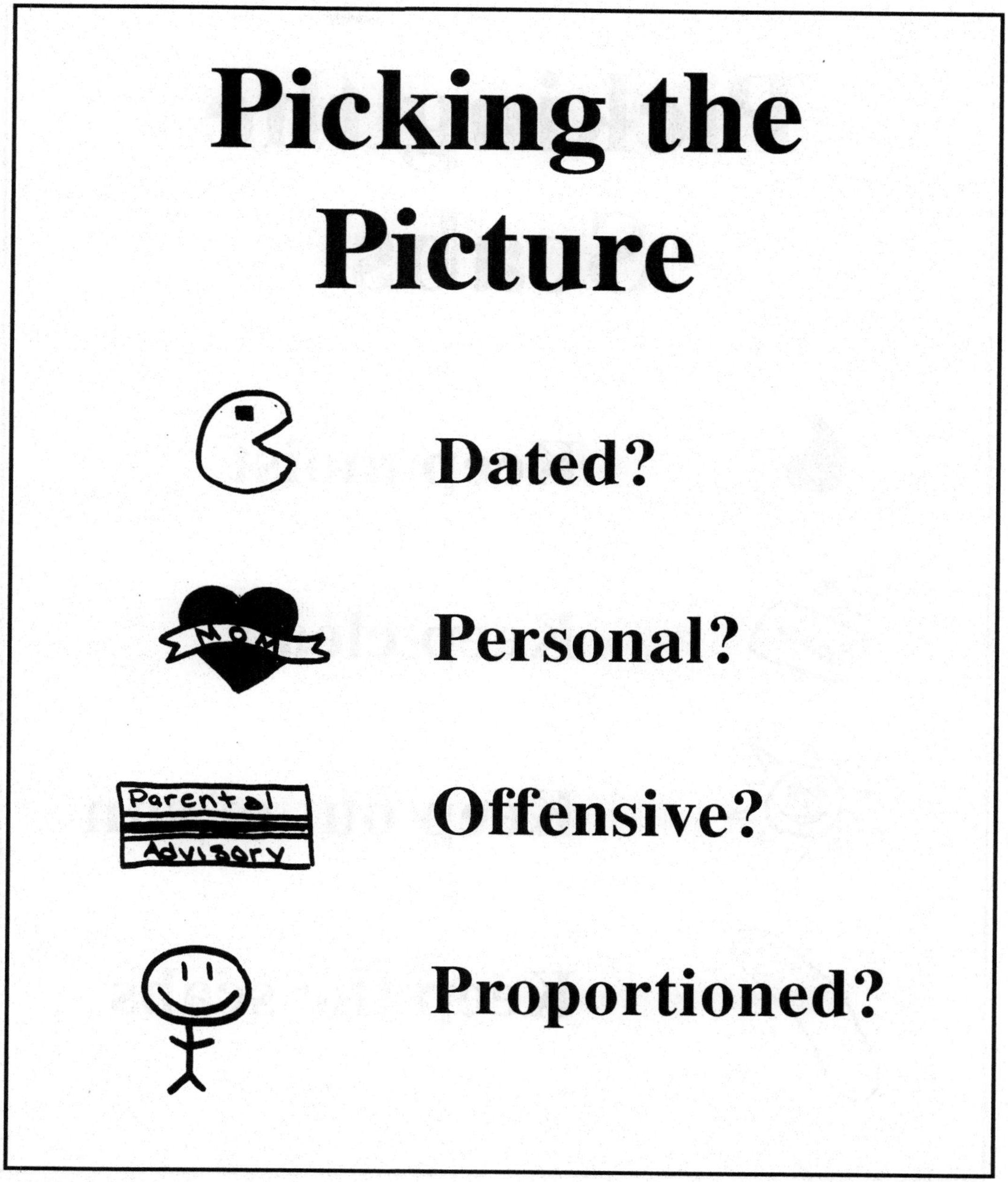

Picking the Picture

 Dated?

 **Personal?**

 **Offensive?**

 Proportioned?

FIGURE 5.6

Picking the Scabs

 Keep moist

 **Keep clean**

 **Keep out of sun**

 Keep the scabs

FIGURE 5.7

- **Create an attention-getting title.** The title page of your A/V is an opportunity to make a strong first impression on your audience, to get their attention, and to establish a connection with them. It is usually a good practice to create a catchy two-part title for your speech. If it is appropriate to your topic, look for opportunities to incorporate images as well as words on the title page, or to include bright colors. In the title page for the tattoo presentation, for example, a big red heart and blue banner lettering would attract the audience's attention because they are brightly colored and because they immediately call to mind what a traditional tattoo looks like.

Tips for Using Computer Slides

As mentioned earlier, the tips for using flip charts apply to other types of visual aids as well. However, since PowerPoint slides have emerged as the dominant medium for visual aids today, both in the classroom and the meeting room, it is important to identify some best practices specifically for computer slides. The examples used in this section are from PowerPoint slides for a classroom presentation on graffiti, entitled "Graffiti: Art or Crime." (See figures 5.8 through 5.13.)

- **Limit the information on each slide.** Because it is so easy to include a lot of information on computer slides, it is also easy to create slides that are too complicated or wordy. Don't give in to the temptation to overload slides with information. A good practice is to observe the "6 × 6 rule," which means that no slide should have more than six lines of information, including headings with no more than six words per line. Notice that the third and fifth slides for the graffiti presentation (figures 5.10 and 5.12) include five lines of information, the heading and four bullet points, and that no bullet point uses more than three words. (An exception to the 6 × 6 rule can be made for the slide where the speaker lists sources for the graffiti presentation.)

- **Keep slides simple.** Also avoid the temptation to overload computer slides with gaudy or cluttered visual details. Be careful to avoid templates, backgrounds, clip art, or fonts that may interfere with or detract from the presentation's message. Slides do not have to include elaborate "bells and whistles" to be effective. Notice that the graphic design for images on the graffiti presentation slides (figures 5.9 and 5.11) is simple and straightforward—just four evenly spaced rectangular images under each heading.

- **Select appropriate images.** Remember that images on computer slides should complement and enhance the presentation's message. They should not be merely decorative. Images included in visual aids need to be relevant and appropriate to the point being made. In the second and fourth PowerPoint slides for the graffiti presentation (figures 5.9 and 5.11) the speaker sets up four images as talking points under each heading by showing relevant examples of graffiti that represent different styles and time periods.

- **Select colors carefully.** Dark backgrounds or sharply contrasting color combinations that may be effective for Web page presentations on a computer screen are not always effective, or even visible, as visual aids projected on a large screen. Generally it is best to use a white background for PowerPoint slides, as in the graffiti presentation, and to select colors that complement one another. Whenever possible, test your PowerPoint slides on a large screen before you present them.

- **Double-check spelling.** Even with a computer spell-checker it is easy to overlook spelling errors on computer slides. There is a famous anecdote about an important public figure in New Jersey who, after meticulously proofing his PowerPoint slides for a speech on public transportation with the spell-checker, nevertheless mistakenly spelled the word "public" as "pubic" throughout the presentation. In the graffiti presentation, the speaker purposely misspells the headings of his PowerPoint slides, substituting "z" for "s," as a visual device to get the audience's attention, to unify the speech, and to reinforce a point about the role of originality and creativity in graffiti.

At the back of the book, in Appendix A, is another set of PowerPoint slides created as visual aids for a student speech on the topic of plastic pollution in the oceans. Using the tips above for using computer slides effectively, critique the content, organization, and design of these visual aids.

Tips for Using Video

With the ever-increasing number of interesting videos available on resources such as YouTube, it is more and more common, sometimes expected, that speakers will incorporate video material into their presentations. If you plan to include video as a visual aid to your presentation, here are some tips for using it effectively:

- **Make it relevant.** Because so much video is available today, it may be tempting to simply inject a clever video into your presentation to amuse the audience or get their attention. But it is important that video, as with any other visual aid, be relevant to the audience and to the message that you wish to present. Video should not be filler; it should be integral to the purpose of your speech.

- **Keep it brief.** Video should not be the star of the show in your presentation. As any visual aid, video should play a supporting role, helping to illustrate and reinforce your message. Therefore, video should take up only a small portion of the time allotted for a presentation. For most classroom presentations, a video clip should run for less than one minute. If it is longer, edit it to focus on specific material you want to highlight.

- **Preview it.** Unless you plan to use video for a surprise effect, preview it for the audience before screening it. Provide a brief introduction or overview of the content and suggest what the audience should watch for. Without spoiling or compromising the impact you wish to make, help the audience understand why you are including the video or how it relates to your presentation's message.

- **Integrate it.** To make best use of the video try to integrate its content or message throughout the presentation, rather than using it as a one-and-done curiosity or exhibit. Explore multiple layers of meaning in the video, pointing out details that may not be immediately apparent or interpretations that the audience may not have considered. If the content is central to your topic, you may be able to use it to reinforce more than one talking point or to provide a striking conclusion for your presentation.

- **Don't talk over it.** If you introduce the video effectively, you do not need to talk while it is screening. Let the audience focus on it without distractions, and hold your comments or analysis until afterward.

Tips for Using Handouts

- **Distribute handouts at the end of your presentation.** Passing out materials, including hard copies of computer slides, during your presentation is a double distraction. First, it interrupts the flow of your speech while you are distributing information. Second, it distracts the audience's attention from you and your message. By introducing handouts during your presentation you are unwittingly creating a distraction for the audience.

- **Tell the audience in advance that you will distribute handouts.** It is good practice as well as basic courtesy to inform listeners that you will distribute handouts with additional or more complete information at the end of the presentation. Therefore, people will not have to take extensive notes on material you have already prepared to give out.

- **Preview and introduce handouts.** You should introduce handouts just as if you were presenting that information with visual aids. You can preview handouts either during the speech, as you discuss the specific points they support, or just before distributing them at the end of your speech, at which time you would also review them for the audience as they receive them. (See discussion below on "How to Present with Visual Aids.")

- **Allow time for questions or discussion of handouts.** It is good practice to use handouts as a segue to a question-and-answer or discussion session after your prepared presentation because there will likely be some questions about the handouts anyway. If there is no time for questions or discussion, invite the audience to contact you later if they have questions.

Art or Crime

FIGURE 5.8

FIGURE 5.9

Termz

- Writers/Taggers
- Toys/Suckers
- Hitting/Bombing
- Getting Up/Killing

FIGURE 5.10

FIGURE 5.11

Effectz

- *Property Value*
- *Negativity*
- *Creative Outlet*
- *Pop Culture*

FIGURE 5.12

Sourcez

- Webster's Universal College Dictionary, 1997, Random House
- Panati, Charles, "What's the Origin of *Kilroy Was Here*", 2000, www.straightdope.com
- New York Times, "Who is Kilroy" 1946
- Farrell, Susan, "The Words: A Graffiti Glossary",2006, www.graffiti.org
- Chalfant, Henry, "Subway Art", 1982
- Shannon, Andrew, Personal Reference, 2006

FIGURE 5.13

HOW TO PRESENT WITH VISUAL AIDS

© alexmillos, 2012. Used under license from Shutterstock, Inc.

The suggestions in this section apply specifically to presenting with visual aids where information is written or projected for the audience to see and read, including flip charts, video, and computer slides. (Suggestions for presenting with props are covered earlier in the chapter.)

- **Set yourself before you begin.** Position yourself so you can work comfortably with your visual aids and still make eye contact with everyone in the audience. "Square up" to the audience and check sight lines; be careful not to turn your back to anyone in the audience. Stand with the visual aids at your left side so you can point to the beginning of each bullet point (because we read left to right). You should be in position to touch or point to the A/V comfortably, without stretching or leaning and without having to shuffle your feet.

- **Use your title page.** Take full advantage of your title page in the introduction, especially if you put a lot of effort and creativity into designing it. With all the tension and excitement at the beginning of a presentation, you don't want to forget to mention the complete two-part title. But do not start off by announcing your title. Instead, build the introduction so that it leads up to and features the title. Perhaps include a dramatic flourish to introduce the title.

- **"Preview" headings.** The headings on visual aids separate the major sections of your speech and identify the main ideas you will cover. To help the audience follow the structure of your presentation, you should provide an overview in the introduction, just before you move into the body of the speech, and then *preview* each heading specifically just before you introduce a new page or slide. Previewing provides transitions that help your presentation flow smoothly, both for you and for the audience. Previewing also helps you look good because it sends a subtle message that you are well-prepared. However, to preview headings effectively you need to "know your speech backwards and forwards" and practice with your visual aids.

- **"Clear the page."** This practice complements the previous one. You *preview* the heading before you proceed to a new page; you *clear the page* when the audience can read the new page. In clearing the page you give the audience a very brief overview of the information covered there. You may think that clearing the page is redundant and unnecessary after previewing the heading, perhaps even a bit condescending to the audience. But speeches need repetition. The trick is to vary the transitional phrases you use to preview headings and clear pages. Clearing the page is especially important in a presentation with detailed charts or graphs that may be difficult for the audience to understand at a glance. In such situations if you do not effectively clear information, your visuals may become a distraction as the audience tries to figure them out.

- **Look at the audience, not at the visual aids.** During a typical ten-minute presentation with visual aids a speaker covers about twelve talking points. This means twelve chances of getting caught in one of the biggest traps that visual aids create for the speaker—the trap of speaking to visual aids, not the audience. One strategy to protect against this risk is to learn a technique we call "Look, Touch, Turn, Talk" (LTTT). This technique can help you maximize the benefits of using visual aids and minimize the risk of losing eye contact with the audience. LTTT breaks down the process of presenting with A/V into four separate steps that keep the speaker's attention focused on the audience, not the visual aids. The four steps of LTTT are:

  - LOOK. You have prepared visual aids to keep you organized and on track. So before you begin to talk about each bullet point, take time to pause and look at it and mentally review what you want to say.

  - TOUCH. While looking at the flip chart or screen, touch or point to the bullet you want to discuss. Use your left hand, the one nearer the A/V. Your extended arm serves as a pointer to draw the audience's attention to that bullet.

  - TURN. This is the most important step! While still looking at and touching the bullet point, turn your head and make eye contact with someone in the audience, preferably someone on your far right side.

  - TALK. Do not proceed to this step until you are looking at someone in the audience. Now, return your hands to the up-and-open position, and begin to speak about the bullet you just pointed to.

- **Pause and "reset" after each talking point.** One of the fringe benefits of working with visual aids is that they can provide regularly spaced pauses during a presentation when you can "reset" yourself and focus on effective delivery skills. Each pause is an opportunity to reinforce good presentation habits and eliminate distractions. Pauses are especially useful if you forget to breathe, tend to speak too fast, or use too many vocalized pauses such as "um," and "ah," or "you know."

What's wrong with this picture?

 # CONCLUSION

Imagine that any time you have a speech to present you could bring a friend along to take some of the pressure off you, to give you psychological support, and to help you look good. It is not a bad idea, in fact, to bring along an actual friend to help you change PowerPoint slides or distribute handouts for your presentation. But you can also bring along the visual aids themselves as a friend to help you out.

This chapter has provided suggestions for how visual aids can help you become a more accomplished and confident public speaker. So the next time you are called upon to give an important speech or report, bring along an A/V friend, as Michelle did for her speech on "Life on the Backstretch," to help you remember and communicate the fascinating information and insights you want to share with your audience.

TIPS AT A GLANCE FOR PREPARING AND USING VISUAL AIDS

- Use audio/visual (A/V) headings to organize a presentation.
- Keep information on A/V simple and clear.
- Employ the "6 × 6 rule" for each A/V page or slide.
- Develop talking points that are easy to follow and remember.
- Double-check spelling on A/V.
- Select colors and images for A/V carefully.
- Limit or edit video materials.
- Rehearse beforehand with A/V.
- "Preview" A/V headings and "clear the page" when presenting.
- Look at the audience, not A/V, when speaking.
- Practice LTTT (Look, Touch, Turn, Talk).
- Use A/V to reinforce positive presentation skills.

C H A P T E R

Rehearsing a Speech

*"Practice is a key component for making
an effective presentation."*

Wayne is a very bright and diligent engineering student who is used to getting good grades. Yet he was having a problem with his public speaking class. When he presented his first speech, he opened with an interesting anecdote that caught the audience's attention and set up the main points he wanted to cover. But as he continued into the body of his speech, the presentation started to founder. He looked at his note card again and again, but could not seem to find the thread that tied the speech together. He looked frustrated and disappointed that his talking points were not falling into place. Finally, he threw in the towel, cut abruptly to a weak concluding comment, and dejectedly sat down.

During the teacher-student conference after the speech Wayne said he could not understand what went wrong. "I practiced this speech over and over in my head," he said, "and I had it perfectly memorized. I ran through it without a mistake in the car on the way to class."

Wayne had undoubtedly put in a lot of time into learning his speech. But did he make the best use of his time? Should he have practiced the speech differently? Was memorizing it such a good idea?

From that frustrating experience Wayne learned that memorizing a speech may not be the most effective way to practice it. He saw that preparing a speech means more than going over it in his head or reciting it to himself in the car. He realized that he put all his energy into *remembering* his speech, not into *preparing* it, and that he had to rehearse differently if he wanted better results. Consequently, Wayne developed a strategy for rehearsing his presentations and refining his speaking skills, and started getting A's on his speeches.

This chapter offers some strategies and suggestions that can help you rehearse your speeches more effectively, and insure that the terrific speech inside your head will be the one that the audience gets to hear.

 ## WHY REHEARSE?

There is a famous story from ancient Greece about how Demosthenes learned to overcome a serious stammer and become a renowned orator by practicing public speaking with pebbles in his mouth. We might imagine ordinary Athenians who heard this wonderful orator speak in the fourth century B.C., thinking that the gods had blessed him with an exceptional gift, never knowing the pains Demosthenes had taken to overcome his handicap and achieve greatness. Likewise, when we encounter excellent public speakers today—business executives, government officials, teachers, ministers, student leaders, banquet speakers—who seem to connect so effortlessly with their audiences, we may assume that they are simply blessed with natural talent. But chances are that these speakers have achieved success through hard effort and lots of practice.

Like Demosthenes, successful public speakers today also devise strategies to minimize their shortcomings and maximize their strengths. They rehearse their speeches as often as necessary, ideally in circumstances as close as possible to the actual speaking situation. For example, a political candidate preparing an important policy speech would likely bring together her closest advisors for a formal "dress rehearsal" before the actual presentation. They might replicate the physical setting for the speech, including the podium placement, microphones, lighting, and the technology for visual aids. They might recreate audience reactions or questions. Finally, they will almost certainly videotape the speech to critique it closely.

Accomplished public speakers go to such lengths to rehearse their speeches because they know that careful preparation is the surest way to anticipate and correct problems with a presentation and to eliminate obstacles that interfere with effective delivery. They understand that there is a direct correlation between practice and success. Good speakers rehearse because they want to look and feel confident, knowledgeable, and relaxed. And they want it all to look effortless to the audience.

If professional speakers work this hard to rehearse their speeches, then you should too. And although you may not have as many resources as the political candidate, you can come up with strategies that will help you prepare speeches more efficiently and productively than Wayne did at first. Practice may not make your speech perfect, but it will almost certainly make it more effective.

STRATEGIES FOR REHEARSING EFFECTIVELY

The following are ten strategies that can help you prepare and rehearse your speeches efficiently.

Rehearse Early and Often

You don't have to wait until your speech is completed to begin rehearsing. With any kind of training it is best to practice frequently rather than to cram everything in at the last minute. You wouldn't train for a marathon, for example, by trying to run twenty-six miles in one workout a few days before the big race. As you are preparing a speech, look for opportunities at any time to try out your ideas aloud, by yourself or for someone else, just to hear how they sound. As you get closer to finishing, rehearse sections of the speech that you feel are ready. It is especially important to practice the introduction and conclusion of the speech because the audience is likely to remember most the impression you create at the beginning and end of your presentation. (Review suggestions in Chapter 3 about how to prepare and deliver introductions and conclusions.) Allow time for several informal run-throughs a few days before the speech, and for at least one formal, timed dress rehearsal.

Record Rehearsals

Many athletes find that taping training sessions is a valuable tool for improving their performance. If you can record speech rehearsals, you can also improve the chances of success when you actually deliver the speech. A speech coach or a friend may point out that you need to improve your posture or eliminate "ums" and "ahs," but you will get the message immediately if you actually *see* these problems for yourself. The video doesn't lie or coddle you. You see exactly what you look like and sound like to the audience, which is invaluable if you want to improve. To become better public speakers we all need to acknowledge our strengths and weaknesses. From trauma comes truth. (See suggestions in Chapter 11 about how to use video recording for self-evaluation.)

Re-create the Speech Setting

Before your presentation, you should take time to investigate the setting for your speech. Is there a podium or lectern in the room? If so, how close is it to the audience? Will there be a microphone? What visual aids would be most effective in the room? How are the sight lines and the acoustics? During rehearsal try to re-create the setting for your presentation, both mentally and physically. You don't have to be elaborate. For example, you can stack books on a table to simulate a lectern or rehearse beside a wall to simulate a screen for PowerPoint slides.

With the setting of your speech in mind, there are a few basic guidelines you should follow when you rehearse. First, unless you are certain that you will be seated during your presentation (as a participant in a panel discussion, for instance), *rehearse your speech*

FIGURE 6.1
Recreate the setting for a presentation when rehearsing, including practice with
visual aids.

standing up so you will be mindful of your posture, body language, and hand gestures. Also
remember to *project your voice* in "presentation range," not "conversation range," when
you rehearse, especially if you are rehearsing in a small room. It is also good to rehearse
with at least one other person present. A friend or family member can often provide crucial feedback for your speech. Moreover, having someone else there when you rehearse
helps create a sense of an audience. If you don't have anyone to watch you, create an imag-
inary audience. One student, for example, hangs magazine ads on the walls in his room to
represent the audience; another student rehearses her speeches to her cat.

Rehearsing in front of a mirror is a technique you should probably avoid. Some speakers find that using a mirror helps them remember to smile or to use gestures. But many
speech coaches advise against this technique because it often makes people self-conscious
about facial expressions and because it discourages focusing on the audience.

Practice Visualization

Wayne's idea to practice his speech in the car on the way to class is not a bad rehearsal
strategy. We should all try to take advantage of "down time," while driving, walking, ex-
ercising, or riding alone in an elevator, to run through a speech mentally, or even to say it

aloud. Some people find this kind of "mental rehearsal" extremely useful. Most speech coaches, however, would advise speakers like Wayne to also include more structured rehearsal, as described here, that re-creates the speech setting.

One of the most valuable aspects of mental rehearsal is that it provides an opportunity to practice *visualization,* which is picturing in your mind the whole process of presenting a successful speech. (Review the section "Imagine Success" in Chapter 1.) In other words, as you run through the speech in your mind, try to imagine in minute detail the presentation proceeding exactly as you would like it to go. Picture yourself, confident and relaxed, explaining each point clearly and thoroughly, connecting with the audience, incorporating visual aids seamlessly into the presentation, and refusing to let any distracting behaviors interfere with the important message you want to deliver. Imagine the audience attentive and eager to hear your ideas, responding appropriately to subtle nuances of your presentation, and applauding enthusiastically when you finish. The key to effective visualization is the *expectation of positive results.* Visualization should reinforce positive attitudes and actions during rehearsal, which in turn should produce successful results during the actual presentation.

Extemporize, Don't Memorize

Some people believe that learning a speech word for word will help them feel more secure when they deliver it. By memorizing the speech they believe they are ensuring success. But memorizing a speech, as Wayne discovered in his first presentation, can create stress and insecurity that might ensure failure instead. Picture a mound of oranges displayed in the produce section of a supermarket. The display is attractive and functional as long as customers select oranges from the top of the pile. But what happens if someone pulls an orange or two from the bottom? The whole display collapses! The same thing can happen with a memorized speech. The presentation may move along smoothly as long as every part of the memorized text falls in its place. But what happens if you misplace one sentence, or perhaps even one word? Or if you suddenly decide to include a new idea, which may upset the tight order of the memorized text? Or, despite all your efforts, if you draw a complete blank at some point in the speech?

Memorizing a speech is not a good rehearsal strategy because memorizing focuses attention on specific *words,* rather than on *ideas.* And because there are many more words than ideas in even a short speech, there is a greater chance that you may forget or misplace some of those words. For this reason, memorizing a speech actually increases anxiety about public speaking for many people. As Wayne discovered, speakers sometimes worry so much about remembering the words of their speech that they lose track of the message they want to communicate.

Rather than trying to memorize your speech when you rehearse, learn to *extemporize* with it. This means that you work with the main ideas you want to present and practice explaining and illustrating them without planning the actual words you will say. You can also organize visual aids that incorporate these main ideas to help you remember them during the

FIGURE 6.2
Use note cards to help organize and extemporize the main
ideas for a presentation.

presentation. Have confidence that the actual words will come to you when you articulate the ideas, which is what happens all the time in casual conversations. In fact, a goal to strive for is to rehearse a speech so it sounds like *heightened conversation,* well prepared and thought-out, but not with the words locked in. As you clarify the main ideas with arguments and examples, and as you rehearse the speech more often, certain words and phrases may repeat themselves, but ideally they will not become permanently set in stone. There will always be some flexibility in your speech if main ideas, not exact words, are holding it together.

The purpose of rehearsing a speech is to help you put your energy into presenting the speech, not just remembering it. Memorizing a speech is counterproductive to this purpose. It is not a good strategy for preparing a speech, nor an efficient use of your time. A much better strategy is to put time into preparing effective visual aids, and then use them to extemporize your speech.

Here is a brief scenario to dramatize some other risks of memorizing: Imagine you have memorized a ten-minute inspirational speech for an awards banquet. In the middle of the program the master of ceremonies whispers to you, "We're running a little late, so could you please keep you remarks to five minutes." Which part of the speech will you present? The first half, or the last half?

Know Your Speech Backwards and Forwards

Although it is counterproductive to memorize an entire speech, there is a lot of value in learning the main ideas backwards and forwards, even if they are outlined on visual aids. This means that you are literally able to say the main points of your speech in reverse order. If you know the main points of your speech backwards and forwards, under pressure you will feel more confident that the organization of your speech is under control. You will also be better able to make smooth transitions from point to point through the speech and to "preview" headings on visual aids for the audience. Knowing them backwards and forwards basically ensures that the main ideas of your speech, like the words you employ to present them, are not an unstable display of oranges. If you wish, you can pick out and extemporize on any one of the ideas without worrying that the whole structure of the speech will topple.

Practice with Visual Aids

Working effectively with visual aids is often a big challenge for inexperienced speakers. Many people underestimate how much practice it takes to look and feel comfortable with visual aids. Even the basic LTTT technique described in Chapter 5 takes more practice and concentration than you might expect. It looks very easy when done effectively, but it takes practice to make it look easy. During exercises with the flip chart in speech classes, students are always surprised at how much concentration it takes to do LTTT correctly.

When rehearsing a speech, spend some time just practicing with visual aids. Reinforce good habits and skills with visual aids so they become an automatic part of your presentation style. Then, when you deliver your speech, you can concentrate more on the content and on the audience. (Review "Tips for Presenting with Visual Aids" in Chapter 5.)

Identify Trouble Spots

Another reason for rehearsing is to identify trouble spots in a speech and to address them ahead of time. Trouble spots may turn up with either the content or the delivery of a presentation. Under content, for example, the introduction or conclusion may be weak or uninteresting. There may be parts of the speech that are unclear or undeveloped, extraneous or long-winded. There may be organizational problems or awkward transitions. For persuasive speeches, there may be problems with insufficient evidence or illogical arguments. Naturally, it is advantageous for speakers to correct such weaknesses before actually presenting the speech.

Likewise, rehearsing can help speakers identify parts of a speech that may present problems with the delivery. Certain words or sentences may be difficult to pronounce, or parts of the speech may feel too slow or too rushed. There may be spots where it would be good to build in a pause or a broad gesture. And rehearsing provides a good opportunity to monitor and correct distracting behaviors that good speakers try to avoid, such as poor posture, nervous body language, or excessive "ums" and "ahs."

Learn from Mistakes

Mistakes are an important part of the learning process. None of us learns to do anything really well without making mistakes. The best time to make mistakes with a presentation is when you are rehearsing it. Rehearsal provides an opportunity to try new things within a controlled setting, where mistakes never count against you and where you have an opportunity to figure out how and why the mistakes occur. Of course, a video of the rehearsal can be extremely useful for pointing up mistakes. But even if you do not tape rehearsals or do not have someone watch you practice, you should try to "observe" your presentation with part of your mind while you are rehearsing and to note where corrections or adjustments need to be made. Learning from mistakes presupposes that we know what the mistakes are. If you don't hear yourself saying "ums," and no one points them out to you, you will never learn to eliminate them.

Time Your Speech

When your speech is nearly ready, it is important to run through it without interruption and time it. Even if you do not have a strict time limit, you should know within a minute how much time you need to present your speech. Usually it is a good idea to time your speech before it is completely finished, so you can add or delete material as needed before the speech is entirely set. If you are allotted a specific amount of time for your presentation, it is essential to time the speech more than once during rehearsal. Most speakers prefer to keep a speech a bit under the maximum time limit to allow some leeway when they deliver it.

In a speech class or workshop you are usually assigned a specific time limit, or a time range, for a presentation, and you can prepare your speech accordingly. But outside the academic world, speakers are often asked to shorten speeches because of unforeseen circumstances. For this kind of situation it is good to plan ahead where you might condense or expand your speech if necessary, and to practice extemporizing it in somewhat shorter or longer versions. Experienced speakers sometimes prepare their material for an "accordion" speech, which can be squeezed or stretched, depending on how much time they have available.

CONCLUSION

Some of us probably believe that confident, dynamic public speakers possess a unique talent for communicating with audiences, that they are blessed with a special gift from the gods. It is easy to forget that many great speakers work hard to make public speaking look easy. Like Demosthenes with his pebbles, many public speakers develop strategies to enhance their oratorical talent and to eliminate distracting behaviors that interfere with it. They continually practice and refine these strategies. Great public speakers are never too good to rehearse their presentations.

TIPS AT A GLANCE FOR REHEARSING A SPEECH

- Rehearse early and often.
- Record rehearsals.
- Re-create the speech setting.
- Practice visualization.
- Extemporize, don't memorize.
- Know your speech backwards and forwards.
- Practice with visual aids.
- Identify trouble spots.
- Learn from mistakes.
- Time your speech.

Developing Listening and Critiquing Skills

*"Paying attention to other speakers' strengths and weaknesses
helps improve your presentation skills."*

Here's a riddle you probably remember from your grade school days: If an airplane crashes exactly on the border between the United States and Canada, in which country do they bury the survivors? The kids who don't get this riddle right away are the ones who don't listen carefully all the way to the end of the question. They hear *airplane crash* and *bury* and, without paying attention to the last word in the sentence, jump to the conclusion that it's about burying *victims*.

This chapter is about developing listening and critiquing skills. These skills are essential for becoming a better public speaker, as well as for improving communication skills generally. We learn about public speaking not only from experience at the podium but also from experience in the audience. Listening carefully to other people's presentations and observing their strengths and weaknesses are very pragmatic activities for you as an aspiring public speaker because they can help you learn how to improve your own presentations.

CRITICAL LISTENING

As an ice-breaker exercise at the first meeting of a public speaking class or workshop it is fun to pair up participants and ask them to introduce each other to the group. Allow about ten minutes for people to interview each other and find out about their background and interests. Then each person introduces his or her partner to the rest of the class. What makes this ice-breaker especially interesting is one simple restriction: no note-taking allowed, neither for the interview nor the introduction.

Besides helping people in the group get to know one another, this exercise helps them listen more attentively and remember what they hear. When students hear "no notes," some of them typically complain that they cannot remember so much information without writing it down. This reaction is not surprising, as studies show that most of us listen at only about 25 percent of our potential. In fact, most of us will acknowledge from first-hand dealings with friends and loved ones that good listening skills are often woefully lacking in our society.

Critical listening involves more than paying attention to information. A speaker's intonation, facial expression, body language, and emotional nuances often communicate far more powerfully than words. A basic premise of communication theory is that as little as 10 percent of spoken communication depends on *what* we say, and as much as 70 percent depends on *how* we say it. Suppose, for example, the person you are interviewing for the ice-breaker exercise tells you, "I went rock climbing in Yosemite National Park last summer." You will probably understand more about what that experience meant for that person from her facial expression, tone of voice, and body language than from her actual words. Effective listening in this situation means paying attention to the *total meaning* of the speaker's communication, tuning into subtle, nonverbal cues about her rock climbing experience as well as the information conveyed in words.

Critical listening means paying attention to a speech not only to absorb information but also to evaluate it intelligently and learn from it. Critical listening is not a passive activity. In fact, some communication specialists describe the most skilled listeners as "athletic listeners" because they pay attention so *actively*. In addition to lack of attention, other obstacles can undermine or interfere with critical listening. Here is another riddle that demonstrates this point:

> *A man and his son are involved in a serious automobile accident. The father is killed instantly, and the son is seriously injured. Paramedics rush the boy to the emergency room of the closest hospital where the chief surgeon looks at the boy and says, "I can't operate on this child; he's my son." How do you explain this situation?*

The answer to the riddle is obvious if you do not assume that the chief surgeon is male. Similarly, making false assumptions about a speaker or a presentation topic, especially if based on personal prejudices or unfair stereotyping, can be a major obstacle to critical listening.

Communication on the highest levels is always a two-way transaction. To communicate better, whether in public speaking or in private conversations, we need to become more aware of obstacles that interfere with skilled listening and compensate for them. Here is a brief listing of some of the most prominent obstacles to good listening and antidotes to them:

Obstacles	**Antidotes**
making false assumptions	being open-minded
jumping to conclusions	withholding judgment
rehearsing your responses	listening "between the lines"
tuning out	eliminating distractions
nit-picking	listening for main ideas

IMPROVING CRITICAL LISTENING SKILLS

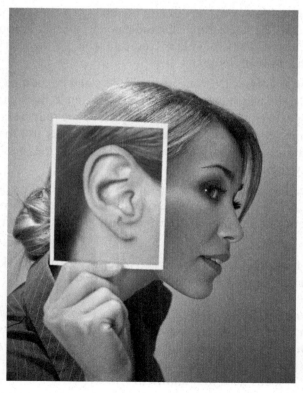

As a participant in a speech class or presentation skills workshop there are some specific measures you can take to develop better critical listening skills. These actions send clear signals to other people at the podium that you are attentive and interested in their presentations. Here are six practical suggestions for becoming a more athletic listener:

- **Assume an attentive listening posture.** As a student of public speaking, you know how body language communicates attitudes. Posture that reflects lack of interest can create or amplify feelings of boredom. Assuming an alert, attentive posture that projects attention and receptivity can actually improve listening.

- **Make eye contact with the speaker.** Eye contact is a crucial element of effective public speaking, both for the speaker and for individuals in the audience. Looking at the speaker is one way people in the audience help make a speech a two-way communication.

- **Find something that interests you.** One of the biggest obstacles to good listening is dismissing the topic or the speaker as uninteresting. If you believe a presentation is going to be deadly dull, it probably will be. A skilled listener can find something interesting or noteworthy about any subject. You can learn something from every presentation, even if only about delivery techniques. What do you see in the presentation that you can use, or avoid, to become a better public speaker?

- **Identify the main ideas.** Pay attention to transitional words and phrases, such as "most importantly" or "therefore," that indicate the speaker is about to state a major point or a conclusion. These "markers" indicate what the speaker considers the highlights of the presentation.

- **Listen between the lines.** Do your best to understand the point a speaker is trying to make, even if he or she is not making it clearly. Listen to more than the speaker's words. Some speakers who are not especially articulate may be communicating a wealth of meaning nonverbally. "Listen between the lines" for the total meaning of the speaker's message, just as you would "read between the lines" to identify subtle meanings in a written text.

- **Be interactive.** Take notes or jot down questions that occur to you during the presentation. Look for ways to use the speaker's message to address your specific needs or concerns. Offer comments or ask questions if there is an opportunity for discussion.

Here's a compact formula for developing active, critical listening skills, courtesy of the Texas A&M University Student Counseling Service:

> *Since you can think faster than the speaker can talk, take advantage of the speed of thought and mentally summarize main points, look for underlying assumptions, anticipate what is coming, evaluate the evidence that is being given, and compare and contrast the [speaker's] ideas with your knowledge.*

OFFERING CONSTRUCTIVE CRITICISM

As a participant in a speech class or workshop you will be expected to critique other people's speeches and suggest ways they might improve them. Many novice speakers feel they are not qualified to evaluate other people's speeches, let alone make suggestions for improvement. But listening attentively to others in your class and giving them helpful feedback is an important responsibility because, in order to improve, every speaker needs to know how his or her speech comes across to the audience. Moreover, learning to give constructive criticism is a skill that goes hand in hand with learning to give good speeches because constructive criticism sharpens your awareness of what works in presentations and what doesn't, ultimately making you more aware of your own strengths and weaknesses. You can learn a lot about good presentation skills by watching other speakers at the podium. There are, however, a few basic ground rules that you must follow when critiquing someone else's speech. Criticism that will be genuinely constructive and helpful for others needs to be *sympathetic, supportive, substantive,* and *specific.*

Sympathetic Criticism

As a speech student, you know how nervous and anxious public speaking can make you feel. So when you critique other students, first of all you need to be sympathetic. They are, after all, in the same boat as you. People react to stress differently. Try to appreciate each speaker's uneasiness and, based on your own experience, suggest ways for him or her to manage anxiety and improve the presentation. The ultimate goal of sympathetic criticism is to help each person become the most effective public speaker possible.

Supportive Criticism

It is important not to undermine a speaker's confidence and self-esteem with comments that are disparaging or derogatory. Phrase your comments in a positive, encouraging way that not only identifies a problem but also suggests a solution. For example, consider these two comments:

> *"Your hand gestures looked nervous and clumsy."*

> *"A lot of nervousness showed in your hands. I think they will look more natural if you use bigger gestures."*

Put yourself on the receiving end of these comments. Both of them convey essentially the same observation that the speaker's hands looked nervous, but there is a world of difference in *how* these statements communicate that observation. The first comment is blunt and demeaning. No one likes to be told they look clumsy. The second comment is not only more supportive but also more helpful because it suggests a way to improve hand gestures.

To be supportive, criticism needs to recognize the speaker's strengths as well as weaknesses. Constructive criticism should always begin with a positive comment about the speaker's presentation. Most people have better chances of improving if they see their weaknesses in relation to their strengths. You are more likely to help the speaker with the nervous hands improve his presentation style if you write a supportive comment like this:

> *"I liked the way you used your hands when you worked with the flip chart. But during the introduction and conclusion I noticed a lot of nervousness in your hands. I think they would look more relaxed if you include broader gestures, like you did with the flips."*

Supportive criticism does not mean that you give only positive feedback. Most people genuinely want to know how they appear to the audience and do not want you to ignore or whitewash weaknesses in their presentation. If you have difficulty hearing a speaker or if you notice the speaker does not make eye contact with you during the speech, you should say so, directly but considerately, in your critique. Such comments are not arbitrary opinions or judgments about the speech; they are observations of physical behaviors you actually noticed. Speakers need such observations in order to improve. Again, put yourself on the receiving end. If several people in the class comment that they could not hear you clearly, you will know to project your voice more to address this problem. If no one comments about it, you don't even know you have a problem.

Substantive Criticism

Even the best public speakers make mistakes when they present. There are no flawless presentations; there are always opportunities for improvement. Most beginning speakers are working to improve several presentation skills at once, but when you evaluate a presentation you should ask yourself, "What can I say that will most help this speaker improve?" In other words, you should try to comment on something *substantive* in the speaker's presentation.

To make speech evaluations more manageable, it is helpful to look at the *content* and the *delivery* of the presentation separately. Under content falls anything to do with the speaker's *message,* including how well the topic pertains to the audience, the overall organization, the effectiveness of the introduction and conclusion, the evidence and examples presented, the information on visual aids, and so on. Under delivery falls anything to do with *how* the speaker conveys the message, including the speaker's interest and enthusiasm, voice projection and speaking pace, posture and body language, eye contact, handling of visual aids, and so on. At the end of this chapter is a "Peer Evaluation Form" that lists observations about content and delivery for evaluating speeches, and also provides spaces for write-in comments. Do not leave theses spaces empty. Your classmates need observations and comments that provide thoughtful, substantive feedback about strengths and weaknesses of their presentations and suggestions for how to improve them.

On the following pages are more abbreviated peer evaluation forms, with only three questions each, about the effectiveness of informative and persuasive presentations. But this evaluation format also addresses key concerns about the content and delivery of a presentation and asks the evaluator to follow up with specific comments and examples. This type of open-ended peer evaluation, which can be easily adapted for different kinds of presentations, is often more valuable for both presenter and audience than a "check list" format because it focuses attention on just a few behaviors. However, if the evaluations are going to help the presenter improve, as an audience member you must make every effort to provide *substantive* comments and examples.

Specific Criticism

Vague comments don't provide much useful feedback for speakers. For example, how helpful would it be to read that "the body of the speech is not clearly organized"? If you were the speaker who received this comment, you would want to know where the organization is flawed and what can be done to improve it. But suppose you receive this comment:

> *"The organization of the first part of your presentation was clear. But I was confused as you started the second section of the speech, where you identify precautions we should take to prevent carbon monoxide poisoning in our homes. I think you need a clearer transition there."*

With this comment, you would understand exactly where the organizational problem lies and how to improve it.

Try to make your comments and suggestions as specific as possible when critiquing a speech. The better you become at identifying specific strengths and weaknesses in others' presentations, the better you will be able to recognize your own.

 CRITIQUING YOUR OWN PRESENTATION

The most difficult presentations to critique are your own. When some people evaluate their speeches, they tend to notice only things that go wrong. But to evaluate a speech fairly we also need to pay attention to what goes right. The best way to improve presentation skills is to concentrate on what works, and build on that. Most importantly, we need to understand *why* things work well or badly in our presentations. To get the most benefits from critiquing your own speech, you need to apply all the listening and critiquing skills you learned from observing other speakers.

Learn from Feedback

In order to develop and improve as a public speaker, you need to assess your strengths and weaknesses honestly. A good starting point is to ask yourself, "How did I feel about this speech?" Review your reactions about a speech while the experience is fresh in your mind. Sometimes you may discover insights about specific moments in a speech. For example, one student wrote in a self-evaluation that she felt "home free" as soon as she got through the introduction and into the first main point of her speech. Another student observed that he "bailed out" in the middle of his presentation because he "felt overloaded with information." Such self-reflection can provide important feedback about how to improve a speech or eliminate impediments to effective delivery.

But to become better public speakers we cannot depend only on self-reflection. We need feedback from other people as well. This is the reason that peer evaluations are such an important part of presentation skills training. The payback for actively listening to and critiquing other people's speeches is that you will receive their feedback when you present. This feedback is vital information, and you should consider it seriously. Carefully review the evaluations you receive from your instructor and your peers, and ask questions when you have conferences with the instructor. Approach every presentation with specific goals in mind, both for the content and the delivery of your speech, and ask your instructor how well you achieved those goals.

If you are giving a presentation outside a classroom or workshop setting, bring a friend or colleague along to observe and comment on your speech. Tell your friend ahead of time what your goals are and what to watch for. In the corporate world it is customary to return this favor when your colleague is making a presentation.

The most valuable source of feedback for any speaker is a video of the actual presentation. Most speech instructors tape their students' presentations because the video provides unfiltered feedback. It does not water down or sugarcoat the truth. The video shows exactly how you look and sound to the audience. Although some students may find the camera intimidating at first, most people quickly learn to focus on the audience, not the camera. But learning to use feedback the camera provides can sometimes be more problematic.

Most people feel uneasy at first seeing themselves on tape in front of an audience, especially if their speech didn't go as well as planned. A typical first reaction is: "That's what I look like? That's how I sound?" Moreover, it is difficult to be objective about your own presentation. But it is important to distance yourself from it and observe your strengths and weaknesses objectively when you watch the video. Usually, it takes a couple of screenings to evaluate your presentation objectively, and perhaps more if you want to zero in on moments that were nerve-wracking or embarrassing. Taking notes as you watch the tape can help you maintain some distance. You can also use the Peer Evaluation Form at the end of the chapter to target specific elements of your speech for closer consideration. Sometimes it's useful to watch the tape with the sound off to see how you look during the presentation. Without sound it is easier to observe physical behaviors and spot problems like nervous body language or awkward gestures. On the other hand, if you just listen to your presentation without watching the screen, it's easier to notice problems with breathing, voice projection, speaking pace, and vocalized pauses like "um" and "you know."

Don't forget to look and listen for good things in your presentation. Remember, to become a better public speaker you need to build on your strengths, not just eliminate your weaknesses.

 ## CONCLUSION

The more you monitor your speaking habits, the more you can improve your communication skills. By reinforcing good habits and eliminating bad habits of your presentations you are learning to communicate more effectively in all kinds speaking situations, from friendly banter to job interviews. So don't just monitor yourself when rehearsing a speech. Finally, remember that learning how to improve speaking skills ultimately ties back in with practicing good listening skills. The more attentively you listen to other speakers, the more you will understand how to command others' attention when you speak.

TIPS AT A GLANCE FOR DEVELOPING LISTENING AND CRITIQUING SKILLS

Listening Skills:

- Remain open-minded.
- Withhold judgment.
- Listen "between the lines."
- Eliminate distractions.
- Listen for main ideas.

Critiquing Skills:

- Provide constructive criticism that is sympathetic, supportive, substantive, and specific.
- Learn from feedback.
- Strive to build on strengths, not just eliminate weaknesses.

PRESENTATION EVALUATION FORM

Presenter: _____

Content

To what extent did the presenter: Very little to a very great extent

- Use an effective introduction to the
  presentation?   1   2   3   4   5
- Make clear the general purpose of the
  presentation?   1   2   3   4   5
- Make clear the specific objectives of the
  presentation?   1   2   3   4   5
- Adapt the information to the audience?   1   2   3   4   5
- Organize the presentation effectively?   1   2   3   4   5
- Use effective devices to maintain interest?   1   2   3   4   5
- Use language appropriate for the audience?   1   2   3   4   5
- Use an effective conclusion to the presentation?   1   2   3   4   5

Specific strengths and suggestions for improving content: _____

_____

_____

_____

Delivery

To what extent did the presenter: Very little to a very great extent

- Show interest and enthusiasm for the topic?   1   2   3   4   5
- Maintain good posture?   1   2   3   4   5
- Maintain effective eye contact with the audience? 1   2   3   4   5
- Use gestures effectively?   1   2   3   4   5
- Control nervous activity?   1   2   3   4   5
- Use visual aids effectively?   1   2   3   4   5

Specific strengths and suggestions for improving delivery: _____

_____

_____

_____

Time _____

INFORMATIVE SPEECH PEER EVALUATION

Presenter: _____

How well did the speaker interest you in the topic? Comment with example.

How well did the speaker organize his/her information? Comment on flip chart.

How might the speaker improve the delivery of this speech? Give specific examples.

PERSUASIVE SPEECH PEER EVALUATION

Presenter: _____

How well were you persuaded to support speaker's proposition? Explain why/why not.

How could the speaker improve the content and delivery of this presentation? Be specific

What improvements have you noticed since the speaker's last presentation?

Developing Speeches that Present Information

"It is best to select a topic that you know about or that already interests you."

In her Environmental Science class Megan is studying ecological problems facing various species of big cats around the globe. She is particularly interested in the cheetah and wants to present an informative speech on this topic for her public speaking class. She has read extensively about the cheetah and has bookmarked many excellent information sources on the Web. But Megan is frustrated because she is having trouble organizing and focusing all this information for a four-to-five-minute speech. She needs a plan to organize the presentation.

Megan's first step is to sort the information and zero in on the topic using a process called mind mapping. (See Figure 2.1.) Circling her topic, "the cheetah," in the center of a blank page, Megan jots down everything that interests her about cheetahs, from the fact that physiologically they are "built for speed" to their solitary "social habits," from the "illegal hunting" and "habitat loss" that threaten them to the "inbreeding" and "low survival rate" of cubs that dramatically increase their "risk of extinction."

After generating ideas on the mind map, Megan draws lines to show how they are interconnected. It becomes clear that Megan's main focus is on the risk of extinction for the cheetah. The mind map has basically helped identify two sets of factors that are driving the cheetah to extinction: one set is "species-related" and the other is "environmental." Some points on the mind map, such as "cub survival" and "inbreeding" for example, fit under species-related factors; and others, such as "illegal hunting" and "habitat loss," fit under environmental factors. With this organizational pattern in mind, Megan is able to put together an interesting five-minute informative speech on the cheetah.

DEVELOPING AN EFFECTIVE INFORMATIVE SPEECH

In order to provide some guidelines that can help you organize and develop an effective informative presentation, let's follow step by step how Megan might develop this speech on the cheetah.

Purpose of an Informative Speech

First, we need to understand the basic purpose of an informative speech. Unlike a "persuasive" speech, whose purpose is to persuade listeners to think or act in a specific way, the purpose of an "informative" speech is to present information clearly. A persuasive speech is a "sales pitch," whereas an informative speech is a "mini lecture." In an informative speech Megan's purpose will be to inform the audience about factors driving the cheetah to extinction, not necessarily to *do* anything about them. If she urges the audience to donate money to "Save the Cheetah Fund" or to join an environmental organization dedicated to preserving the cheetah, then her presentation becomes a persuasive speech, which is the focus of another chapter.

Of course, separating information and persuasion in a speech is an artificial distinction that does not exist in most real-world speaking situations, where the purpose of a presentation is often both to inform *and* persuade the audience. After all, if you feel passionate about a topic like the extinction of the cheetah, why wouldn't you try to persuade the audience to take action to prevent it? But to organize and develop effective presentations, it is useful to address the specific goals and objectives of informative speeches and persuasive speeches separately.

Selecting a Topic

Megan is fortunate to begin with a general topic already in mind. For an informative speech it is best to select a topic that you know about or that already interests you. Virtually any topic can work for an informative presentation. It may be serious or light-hearted, familiar or exotic, practical or philosophical.

You can draw on personal experience to find a topic that may be uniquely suited to your background or interests. Megan's topic emerged from a personal interest in cheetahs that began in her Environmental Science class. You should also look for a topic that relates to your own experience. If you have asthma, talk about "Living with Asthma." If you enjoy sky diving, talk about "Parachuting: An Extremely Safe Extreme Sport." There are many ways to establish a personal connection with a topic. Perhaps you don't have asthma, but your cousin or best friend does. You may not have actually tried sky diving, but your friends are urging you to join them for their next jump. The point is that an informative speech topic will be more interesting and engaging for the audience if you identify a personal connection with it. (See Chapter 2 for additional suggestions about selecting a speech topic.)

Narrowing the Topic

Once you have a general topic in mind, you can use brainstorming or mind mapping to focus it more specifically. A good way to narrow your topic is to plan visual aids early on, identifying headings and bullet points for the speech. This strategy can help you sort through information, decide what's important, and focus your material for a specified time limit. Megan probably has enough information to talk about cheetahs for at least ten minutes, so she needs to limit the material for a five-minute speech by eliminating anything that doesn't directly relate to species-related or environmental factors driving the cheetah to extinction.

Researching the Topic

No matter how much personal experience you have about a topic, to be credible and effective in an informative speech you need additional outside information to complement your experience. Choosing a topic that you are knowledgeable or passionate about does not automatically make you an expert on it. To ensure success with an informative speech you must do some research. How much research and what kind of resources you need may depend on the topic, the assignment, or the setting and time limit of the presentation. For example, Megan researched information about cheetahs from several kinds of resources, including her Environmental Science textbook, her instructor's lecture notes, scholarly articles about endangered species, current newspaper articles about cheetahs, and many websites ranging from cheetah preservation societies to zoos. Megan is required to include research from at least four sources in her presentation, but she plans to cite five or six sources.

For an effective informative speech, however, you need to be concerned not only about how much information to include but also about the *quality* of that information. Today, information about important issues is continually updated. Some online news services update their websites atleast every hour, for example, and more frequently with fast-breaking news stories. Therefore, in researching a speech you should look for information that comes from sources that are current and recognized as accurate, reliable, and knowledgeable about your topic. (Review Chapter 2 for suggestions about researching a topic and evaluating the accuracy and reliability of researched information.)

Finally, you need to recognize certain ethical issues when researching material for an informative speech. Information should not only be clear and well-organized but also honest and well-balanced. For example, Megan would not want to mislead the audience—even unintentionally—about the plight of the cheetah by changing, manipulating, or leaving out relevant information about its risks of extinction. And, even though she is very knowledgeable about this topic, Megan should not rely on memory but should check the accuracy of her information before the speech. And, of course, she is obliged to attribute credit to her information sources during the presentation.

Organizing and Outlining the Speech

You've narrowed your topic and done some research, and you have identified the main ideas, or headings, you want to cover in your speech. So now it's time to outline specific talking points. For a five-minute speech Megan figures there will be time to develop and explain about three or four points under each heading. Megan creates an outlines for her presentation, which will also serve as the headings and bullet points for her visual aids:

Species-Related Factors

- Loss of genetic diversity
- Solitary social habits
- Low survival rate for cubs

Environmental Factors

- Competition for food
- Loss of habitat
- Illegal hunting

Allowing for a well-developed introduction and conclusion, Megan cannot effectively address more than these talking points within the five-minute time limit. On paper, this looks like an interesting, focused informative presentation.

When organizing your speech, you may have to be selective, even ruthless, about editing the bullet points. A specified time limit can often help you organize a presentation by forcing you to fit the outline to the time frame. This strategy is especially useful if you have a lot of information or if you are reluctant "to throw anything away." But don't try to cover too much; focus your presentation on the most important information.

Creating a Title

Even if you are not using visual aids for your speech, you should create a title for it, preferably a two-part title that presents the main topic and also identifies a specific perspective on it. A catchy, engaging title is a good way to get the audience's attention, arouse their curiosity, and connect with them. For her speech Megan decided early on that the word "extinction" would be in the title. Finally, by juxtaposing two ideas from her mind map, she comes up with a perfect two-part title for this speech:

The Cheetah:
Sprinting toward Extinction

It's worth taking time to create an imaginative two-part title for your informative speech, especially if your topic is not particularly dramatic or exotic. Here are three examples of two-part titles that hint at interesting informative presentations:

Sign Language:
A Word in the Hand

Imaginative Play:
The Building Blocks of Learning

Anorexia Nervosa:
Are You Starving for Attention?

Developing Visual Aids

Megan will be using three flip-chart pages as visual aids for her presentation: a title page with her two-part title and two information pages with the headings and bullet points outlined above. Although she is not especially artistic, Megan has some creative ideas for the flip chart to reinforce her topic and stimulate the audience's interest in it. She plans to color the letters of the main title, "The Cheetah," light brown with black spots to suggest the cheetah's distinctive markings, and to print the word "Extinction" so that it begins with large, thick black letters that gradually become thin and fade away by the end of the word. Megan also plans to use bright colors in the headings on the information pages and cheetah paw prints as bullets for the talking points. Although these graphic enhancements are not necessary, Megan incorporates them to help the audience remember her message about the cheetah.

The most important considerations in designing visual aids for an informative presentation should be clear focus, organization, and continuity. Graphics on visual aids generally enhance informative presentations, as long as the design elements do not interfere with or detract from the tone of the presentation. For example, humorous clip art on visual aids for a serious topic such as teen suicide would be counterproductive and in bad taste. (Review Chapter 5 for a full discussion of how to prepare and use visual aids.)

Introduction and Conclusion

For the introduction for her speech Megan should take advantage of her personal experience about how she became aware of the plight of the cheetah in her Environmental Science class. She might mention a few details and statistics that first aroused her interest in cheetahs, such as low survival rates for cubs or the devastating impact of poachers on the species. These details will also help Megan establish speaker credibility, since they indicate to the audience that she has done research on this topic. To further reinforce her credibility, Megan might present a quote from a reputable source about the threat of extinction for cheetahs. And, of course, she should communicate her deep interest in this topic. Finally, Megan should introduce the topic by making the purpose of the speech clear, by connecting the topic to the audience, and by presenting the two-part title on the first flip-chart page.

Megan should incorporate these same elements in her conclusion, but in reverse order. She should wrap up the main points in a way that best reinforces her message about the dangers cheetahs face, reiterate her personal interest in this topic, and reprise her two-part title in a way that will leave the audience pondering the cheetah's plight, sprinting toward extinction.

CRITIQUING AN INFORMATIVE SPEECH

Now let's look at how these strategies work in an actual informative presentation. Read the transcript of the speech below about "Weight Watchers," keeping in mind how the speaker has organized and focused the information on this topic. This is a student presentation for an assigned informative speech, four to five minutes long, that incorporates personal experience and information from at least three outside sources. It employs three flip-chart pages as visual aids. Figures 8.1 through 8.3 show the visual aids the speaker prepared for this presentation. After you have read the speech, you will find observations and commentary about it.

Weight Watchers:
Lose Weight and Get in Shape

by Leah Ciurczak
RVCC Student

1   Good morning, everyone. I'm glad to see you all here this morning. From the time I was a young girl, I was never too concerned about what or how I ate. But as I got older, the food choices I made were catching up with me. Gradually, I began to notice, as perhaps some of you have too, a steady increase in my weight and a decrease in my desire to exercise. I talked with a friend who was facing the same situation, and together we decided to search out a healthy and effective weight-loss program. We decided to join Weight Watchers. I have been a member of the program for two years now, and have lost close to fifteen pounds. Today, I would like to tell you a little about Weight Watchers, how it works and why it is an effective way to lose weight and get in shape.

2   First, I'd like to talk about what Weight Watchers is. Weight Watchers is a weight-loss company that was founded in the 1960s and, according to Wikipedia, is now active in more than thirty countries worldwide. The most important aspect of Weight Watchers is that it is a support group for people who want to control their weight and are willing to make a long-term commitment to it. People who become members of Weight Watchers are required to weigh in at specific locations. There are regular meetings at these locations, comprised

FIGURE 8.1

What is it?

- Support Group
- Diet Products Provider
- Way of Life

FIGURE 8.2

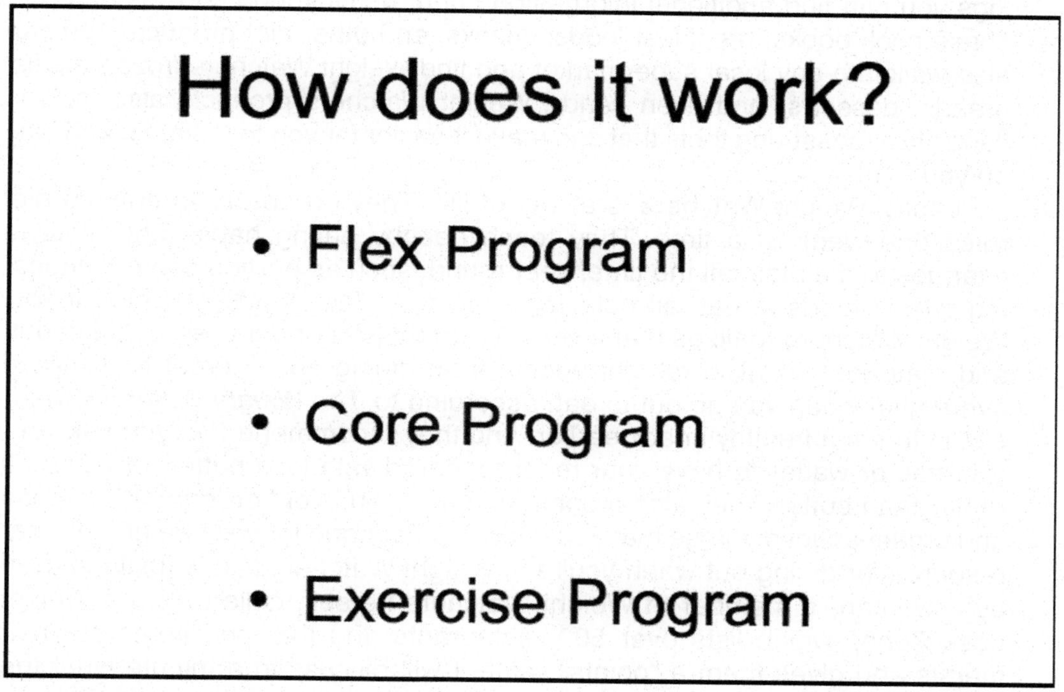

FIGURE 8.3

of individuals who are going through similar experiences with weight control. And although members are not required to attend the meetings, these groups do provide a lot of support and motivation. And there are counselors available there who are willing to talk with you about anything at any time.

3   Weight Watchers is also a diet products provider. At Weight Watchers meetings you can find additional information about healthy food choices and purchase cook books, breakfast foods, snacks, and other diet products. You can also walk into any local supermarket and find Weight Watchers frozen meals, breads, desserts, and even candy. Weight Watchers products also include things like measuring tools that can make it easier for you to maintain and stay on your diet.

4   Lastly, Weight Watchers is a way of life. They do not try to enforce diet rules one week at a time. They teach healthy eating habits and lifestyle changes to maintain all the time, year round, such as portion control, choosing proper foods to eat, and staying away from fatty foods and fried foods. Weight Watchers realizes that a very important part of our lives is dining out, and they don't want to restrict people from dining out. A great tip to avoid overeating when you go out to eat, according to *The Weight Watchers Manual,* is to eat a healthy snack earlier. And they recommend that you ask your waitress or waiter to have your meal prepared with less butter, or using oil rather than butter. They also recommend that you avoid ordering fried foods and cream sauces, things that you know are not good for your weight. A great resource for dining out when you're in Weight Watchers is a website started by a woman, a member of Weight Watchers herself, called "Dotti's Weight Loss Zone," which lists over 500 restaurants and the food items on their menus and gives them a "points" value. I will discuss in a minute what the points value means, but for now just know that it's very important to those of us who are in Weight Watchers and still enjoy dining out.

5   I would now like to discuss how Weight Watchers works. Weight Watchers is based around two main programs. The first is the Flex Program. This used to be called the Points Program, which is a method for calculating points. When you attend your first Weight Watchers meeting, you are assigned a point value, that is, how many points you are allowed to eat during the day. You can eat anything you like, anytime during the day, as long as you stay under this number of points. And that's why it's called the Flex Program, because it's flexible.

6   The second program is called the Core Program. This program was created to compete with the low-carb diets that were a fad a few years ago. Weight Watchers lists many foods that are considered core foods. These are very healthy foods, such as fruits and vegetables, lean meats, and low-fat dairy products. They say that you can eat as many of these core foods as you want, as long as you are eating to feel satisfied and not full.

7   Lastly, Weight Watchers does highly recommend a good exercise program. Exercise, as we all know, is a very important aspect of any weight-loss program. Exercise helps you lose weight faster, it helps you tone your body, it helps you gain energy and also gain confidence.

8   And now that you know a little bit about what Weight Watchers is and how it works, you may realize that it's time for you to make some healthy life-style decisions, just as I did. It may help if you confide in a friend and check out Weight Watchers together as a way to motivate you and provide an incentive to lose weight. At least now you are more informed about one of the many weight-loss programs out there. Weight Watchers, a great way to lose weight and get in shape!

Sources

"Dotti's Weight Loss Zone," http://www.dwlz.com/restaurants.html.
"Weight Watchers," *Wikipedia, The Free Encyclopedia,* http://en.wikipedia.org/wiki/Weight Watchers.
"Welcome to Weight Watchers," *The Weight Watchers Manual,* p. 19.

Let's take a closer look at this "Weight Watchers" speech and analyze how Leah organized and focused the information for this presentation. The following are some noteworthy features of this speech.

Topic Selection

Leah has obviously selected a topic that she already knows a lot about, having been a member of Weight Watchers for two years and having already lost close to fifteen pounds in the program. She establishes a personal connection with the topic by including first-person references to Weight Watchers in the introduction and conclusion, as well as in paragraph 4 of the speech. She has narrowed the topic down to two specific questions about the Weight Watchers program: What is it? and How does it work?

Two-Part Title

Leah has devised a two-part title for the presentation: "Weight Watchers: Lose Weight and Get in Shape." Although this title may not be as catchy as the one for Megan's presentation on the cheetah earlier in the chapter, it is succinct and defines a clear focus for the speech. The headings identify the results successful Weight Watchers members hope to achieve. The second part of the title suggests that the Weight Watchers program encourages its members to "take control" of their weight and their life choices.

However, by tying in more with some material in the body of this presentation, Leah could probably create a more interesting, colorful title for this speech. There are several good cues for a catchier title in this speech. For example, consider the beginning of paragraph 4: "They [Weight Watchers] do not try to enforce diet rules one week at a time. They teach healthy eating habits and lifestyle changes to maintain all the time. . . ." Can you think of a catchy title that might emerge from these lines? Try juxtaposing the most dynamic words and phrases in these sentences. For example:

Weight Watchers:
Not Diet Rules, but Healthy Eating Habits

Or consider a title that plays off the interesting website mentioned in paragraph 4:

Weight Watchers:
Keeping You in the Weight-Loss Zone

Organization and Visual Aids

For the most part Leah has organized information for this speech clearly and efficiently under the two headings, which are presented as questions. We see that the information in each paragraph of the speech matches the bullet points on the visual aids, and that Leah has included a segue at the beginning of paragraphs 2 and 5 to *preview* each new heading. Interestingly, in her original outline for this presentation, Leah included the material about "Dotti's Weight Loss Zone" under the "Support Group" bullet, since it provides a good example of online support for Weight Watchers. But she decided to use this information instead to reinforce the section about dining out under the "Way of Life" bullet, where it can also serve as a transition to the "Flex Program" bullet on the next page.

The organization of the visual aids is simple and straightforward. Leah has outlined three talking points for each heading and limited each bullet to two or three words. She has kept the wording of the bullets parallel, especially on the last page with the repetition of "Program." The bullets under the heading "What Is It?" are effective because they build up to the most interesting feature about Weight Watchers, that it is a "way of life."

Quality of Information

The information in this presentation is adequate to cover the topic and to meet the time limit of four to five minutes. The bullet points are fairly well developed, except for the final one about "Exercise Program." In comparison with the other key points in this speech, especially the first three, this last point is too general. Paragraph 7 needs more information or comments about the exercise program Weight Watchers recommends.

The quality of the information in this speech is also appropriate for the presentation, although the speaker could make the content more interesting in some places. There are basically three kinds of information presented in this speech:

- Information that provides *facts* about the topic, such as when Weight Watchers was founded and how active it is worldwide.
- Information that provides *supporting details or examples,* such as examples of "healthy eating habits and lifestyle changes" or of healthy "core foods."
- Information that provides *recommendations or "tips"* for weight control, such as suggestions for healthy diet practices while dining out.

To enhance the quality of information Leah might add a few more personal impressions or comments about the Weight Watchers program, especially in the body of the speech. For example, in a question-and-answer session after this speech, someone would be likely to ask, "Can you tell us more about how you lost the fifteen pounds?" Or perhaps, "What did you think the first time you attended a Weight Watchers meeting?" Leah could also enrich the information in this speech by incorporating a few direct quotes. For example, a quote from the friend who joined Weight Watchers with her would provide an additional source of information as well as another perspective to complement Leah's personal experience with the program.

There are also a few places where information in this speech is not quite clear or specific enough. For example, in paragraph 5 where Leah explains the flex program as "a method for calculating points," the audience would probably like to know more specifically *how* these points are calculated. One simple supporting example here might easily clear up any ambiguity. For instance, how many points is an ounce of butter worth, as compared with an ounce of carrot sticks? Likewise, the last sentence of paragraph 6 is likely to be unclear for the audience. What exactly does it mean to say, "eating to feel satisfied and not full"? And the information at the end of paragraph 2 would be more useful if it were not so general: "And there are counselors available there who are willing to talk with you about anything at any time." This point could be improved by choosing words more specific than "anything" and "any time," or by providing an example.

Incorporating and Citing Research

Leah has fulfilled the requirements for the informative speech by citing three outside sources on Weight Watchers. These appear to be reliable sources that provide information about the program from different perspectives. The most useful sources of information are *The Weight Watchers Manual* and the website for "Dotti's Weight Loss Zone," cited in paragraph 4, the most interesting and fully developed part in the presentation. The information in this paragraph is probably what the audience will remember most from this speech.

On the other hand, the least developed part of this speech, as mentioned, is paragraph 7, which addresses the importance of exercise. If Leah decided to include additional research in the presentation, this would be the place to add it. Because the two-part title suggests that to "get in shape" is an important outcome of the Weight Watchers program, Leah should provide more supporting information for this point in the body of the speech. An additional quote, statistic, comment, or "tip" about exercise and Weight Watchers would strengthen this point.

When gathering and evaluating research for an informative speech, it is important to look at the distribution of research throughout the presentation. To be effective you should reinforce every major point with specific information, examples, or explanation from outside sources. Personal experience is a valuable asset in an informative presentation, especially one like the Weight Watchers speech where the speaker's experience is so closely tied in with the topic; but researched information from authoritative sources always adds substance and credibility. An ideal topic for an informative speech is one where there is balance between personal experience and research that complement one another.

Introduction and Conclusion

In the introduction to this speech Leah uses personal experience effectively to get the audience's attention and to establish credibility. Notice especially the sentence where she says: "Gradually, I began to notice, *as perhaps some of you have too,* a steady increase in my weight and a decrease in my desire to exercise." This sentence is the key to this introduction. Very simply and unobtrusively, Leah establishes a connection with the audience by including them in her personal concerns about weight control. The final sentence in the introduction states the purpose of the speech and allows Leah to use her two-part title as a transition into the body of the speech.

In the conclusion of the presentation Leah again connects her topic, and her personal experience, with the audience: "And now that you know a little bit about what Weight Watchers is and how it works, *you may realize that it's time for you to make some healthy life-style decisions, just as I did.*" This statement wraps up the presentation, by reiterating the two main headings about Weight Watchers, and reinforces the speaker's interest in the topic by including the phrase "just as I did" at the end. Leah concludes by restating her two-part title and, judging from the exclamation point at the end, delivering it with emphasis.

The introduction and conclusion of this speech complement each other. Leah draws on personal experience to connect the topic with the audience at the beginning and the end of the presentation. One opportunity to make the introduction and conclusion more engaging might be for Leah to include some details about her friend, or perhaps a quote from her, in order to bring in the friend's personal experience as well.

 **CONCLUSION**

The purpose of this chapter is to provide practical guidelines and suggestions to help you organize and develop an effective informative speech. By following the development of Megan's speech about cheetahs and analyzing Leah's Weight Watchers speech, you hopefully have a better understanding of the process of how to build an informative presentation that can have an impact on your audience and allow you to feel that you have made some difference in their lives.

TIPS AT A GLANCE FOR DEVELOPING SPEECHES THAT PRESENT INFORMATION

- Select a topic that you already know or that interests you.
- Narrow the topic by brainstorming or mind mapping.
- State the purpose of your presentation.
- Use visual aids to plan and organize your speech.
- Incorporate personal experience.
- Research information from reliable sources.
- Present information that covers the topic adequately, supports each main point, and meets time requirements.
- Present information that it is current, accurate, and relevant.
- Create a two-part title.
- Prepare an introduction that engages the audience, establishes speaker credibility, and connects the topic with the audience.
- Prepare a conclusion that wraps up the topic, reinforces your interest in it, and leaves the audience thinking about it.
- Cite sources of information during the presentation.

Handling a Question-
and-Answer Session

*"The Q&A session is an opportunity to build
on your prepared presentation."*

Bill is very passionate about environmental issues. And because he is concerned about the impact of automobile exhaust on the earth's atmosphere, he wants to speak about "Bio-Diesel: An Alternative to Gasoline" for his final presentation in speech class. He has been reading about this topic for months, and he thinks it will make an effective final speech. But since he is not very technology-oriented and knows little about car engines, Bill is worried that in the question-and-answer session after the speech he will be asked a lot of highly technical questions about bio-diesel that he won't know how to answer, especially since there are several students in the class who are car buffs. He doesn't want to look foolish or uninformed in the Q&A discussion, particularly for a subject that is so important to him.

Bill needs a strategy to help him prepare for the Q&A session and bolster his confidence for this presentation topic. He decides there are two things he can do:

First, before the presentation Bill will look at his speech from the audience's perspective and try to anticipate where his classmates are most likely to have questions. He will prepare these sections especially well, and even reserve a few bits of information as extra information for the Q&A session.

Second, Bill has an article from a scientific journal that describes in great technical detail how bio-diesel fuel works, how ordinary diesel engines can be modified to burn it, and the advantages of developing bio-diesel as an alternative to gasoline. Naturally, Bill intends to use parts of this article for his presentation, but he also plans to bring it with him for the Q&A discussion as a reference source he can pass along to anyone who is interested in technical details about bio-diesel.

Knowing he has reserve information and a definitive resource about bio-diesel close at hand for the Q&A session helps Bill feel more secure about fielding questions on his topic and generally more confident going into the presentation. In fact, the questions the audience asked were easy for Bill to answer because they focused mostly on practical concerns: "What's it like to drive a car that runs on bio-diesel?" "Is there someplace nearby where you can purchase bio-diesel fuel?" The only technical question that came up was exactly about the material Bill had prepared, so he looked very knowledgeable with additional information and resources right at his finger tips. The Q&A session for Bill's speech was a great success because he prepared for it effectively.

The purpose of this chapter is to help you prepare for questions about your topic, handle them more effectively during the presentation, and generally bolster your confidence about that part of your presentation that is most difficult to plan for—the question-and-answer session.

STRATEGIES FOR HANDLING Q&A

Start with the Right Mind-Set

What if you could dial up one of those psychic hotlines you see on television to find out what your audience really wants to know about your speech topic? That is exactly what you will discover in the question-and-answer session. If you are well prepared for your presentation and follow a few basic guidelines for handling questions presented in this chapter, you will find that the Q&A session is a great asset to your presentation, an opportunity to enhance your message and your image, rather than a liability to be dreaded or avoided. Try to approach the Q&A with this mind-set.

The following are some basic guidelines that should help make the question-and-answer session a positive experience, both for you and the audience.

Prepare for Q&A

This handbook has encouraged you to prepare carefully for every aspect of your presentation in order to feel confident and in control when you deliver it. But one part of the presentation that you cannot completely control is the question-and-answer session because you cannot be certain what questions the audience will ask. This uncertainty makes some people uneasy about Q&A. Yet there are simple, effective strategies you can use to maintain reasonable control even over the Q&A session.

You can begin to establish control over Q&A long before you deliver the speech. When you are planning and rehearsing your presentation, anticipate questions that the audience is likely to ask about your topic. For example, if your speech is about sky diving, you can be fairly certain that someone will want to know how it feels to look down from the airplane just before you jump. Typically, audiences are most likely to ask questions about the speaker's personal experiences related to the topic or about unusual information mentioned in the presentation. They are also likely to ask about aspects of the topic that are extraordinary or controversial. So part of your normal speech preparation should be to bone up well on questions like these about your topic. You should keep in reserve some additional examples or information about them for the Q&A session, anticipating that there will be questions. As you prepare your speech, ask yourself what questions you might raise about your topic. What response would best satisfy these questions? What kind of response would make you look good? You might even rehearse answers to questions you expect to come up.

Announce When You Will Take Questions

Another way to establish control over the question-and-answer session is to decide in advance when you will take questions. You should tell the audience how and when you will take questions. There are basically two choices, either during or after your presentation. If you feel comfortable taking questions as they arise, tell your listeners they can "feel free to ask questions at any time," or pause from time to time and ask if there are any questions. This type of Q&A is generally effective for longer presentations or for those that do not have strict time limitations. Teachers typically use this approach in presenting a lecture or lesson. By taking questions during your speech you break up the presentation and give the audience an opportunity to interact with you. Let the audience know when you are ready for questions. For example: "Before we go on to discuss the preliminary planning for this project, are there any questions about the demographic research I just covered?"

If you prefer not to answer questions during your presentation, tell the audience that you "will be happy to take questions at the end" of your speech or that you "will leave time for questions" after the formal part of your presentation. In fact, audiences generally expect that the Q&A will come at the end of the presentation, especially in speech classes or workshops, so in these situations you do not need to mention Q&A until you are actually ready for questions. But you need to provide a segue into the question-and-answer session. The best practice is simply to announce that you are ready to take questions.

Set Guidelines for Q&A

As a public speaker you are in a power position at the podium. You establish the tone and the format for the presentation. When you open the floor to questions, you are in effect sharing this power with the audience, but you are still the one who controls the discussion. You do not have to recognize individuals unless they follow guidelines you set. Keep this basic principle in mind if you are worried that the question-and-answer session may get heated or out of control.

So, you determine how you will recognize questions from the audience. If the presentation is informal or you feel comfortable with the audience, you may simply ask, "Are there any questions?" If the audience is large or if you expect many questions, you should *raise your hand* as you announce that you will take questions. This simple gesture will signal the audience that you will recognize people who raise their hands (in an orderly way) rather than those who shout out (in a disorderly way).

Remember that audiences sometimes need a little time to formulate questions. So be prepared to wait a few seconds at the beginning or to get Q&A started yourself. Two simple things you can do are:

- **Ask yourself a question.** "Some of you may be wondering what the time line is for installing these new computers."
- **Have a classmate or colleague ask a question you've prepared ahead of time.** In the business world it is not uncommon for colleagues to support one another at presentations by asking a "soft" question to get Q&A rolling, especially if the question follows up on a point that may need further clarification or explanation.

Remember that Q&A Belongs to Everyone

So, you have a question from the audience. What do you do now? The first thing you should do is listen carefully and make eye contact with the person asking the question. Give the questioner your full attention. If the setting allows, move a few steps closer. When you have heard the question, it is good practice to repeat it or paraphrase it for the audience. This is especially important for a larger audience, partly because some people may not have heard the question but more importantly because paraphrasing an individual's question makes it the *group's* question. It now belongs to everyone, and you can avoid getting involved in an extended one-on-one dialogue just with the questioner.

As you begin to answer the question, maintain eye contact for a few more seconds, but as you continue the answer, look at other individuals in the audience, again to involve more people and to reinforce that you are answering this question for the group, not only for the individual who posed it. When you finish, turn your attention to another section of the audience to encourage more people to participate in the Q&A discussion. Avoid tagging your answer with, "Did I answer your question?" Spreading your attention around the audience discourages follow-up questions that may cause other people to disengage or tune out. Remember that the question-and-answer session belongs to the entire audience; don't allow a few individuals to monopolize it.

It's best to keep your answers brief and to the point. Long-winded responses often discourage further questions. Whenever possible, connect your answers to the prepared content of your presentation, both because it keeps you on safe ground and because it keeps the Q&A session focused and relevant to your subject.

ANTICIPATING PROBLEM QUESTIONS

What if You Don't Know the Answer?

The biggest concern most inexperienced speakers have about the question-and-answer session is, "What if I don't know the answer to a question?" Some people in this situation might either try to avoid the question completely or make up an answer. Don't make these mistakes! It is always better to be honest and acknowledge when you do not know the answer to a question. If you are caught making up an answer, you lose credibility as a speaker, and probably the audience's respect as well.

On the other hand, one of the cardinal rules of public speaking is that you never let yourself look bad. So, admitting that you do not know the answer to a question is not the best course of action either. Keep in mind that even experts don't know everything about their subject. However, audiences expect experts to know *where to find* answers to relevant questions about their topic. Therefore, when faced with a question you don't know how to answer, the best course of action is to state, without apologizing, that you "didn't come across that information in your research" or you "don't have that information right at hand," *but* that you can find the information or you can direct the questioner to sources that will have it. If other members of the audience also have some expertise on your subject, perhaps you can refer the question to them. If you promise to get back to someone later with additional information, be sure to provide it.

How Can You Diffuse a Hostile Question?

Every speaker's Q&A nightmare is being asked a hostile question. Actually, hostile questions occur much less frequently than you might imagine because most people are uncomfortable with confrontational situations and therefore tend not to ask confrontational questions, sometimes even if they disagree strongly with the speaker's position. But if you should encounter a hostile question, there are five things you can do to defuse it:

- **First, don't lose your composure.** The worst thing you can do is reinforce the questioner's hostility by losing your temper or trying to put the person down. The audience will be on your side as long as you remain composed and professional.

- **Second, take care to rephrase the question in neutral terms.** For example, someone asks: "Why the hell are you cutting the budget on this project again when any idiot can see that it needs a 20 percent increase?" You paraphrase like this: "The question is why a budget cut is necessary on the project at this time." By rephrasing the question in neutral terms you not only take the sting out of a hostile question, you also present it to the audience in a way that you can respond to reasonably on your own terms, not on the questioner's.

- **Third, acknowledge the questioner's position.** A hostile question may in fact be raising a legitimate point of opposition. Acknowledge it before you begin your answer: "The question raises an important point. I know we all want this project to succeed, but there are good reasons to cut back on the budget right now. Let me explain them briefly."

- **Fourth, avoid eye contact with the hostile questioner.** Take your time responding to a hostile question to show you are keeping your cool, taking the question seriously, and preparing a thoughtful answer. When you feel composed, glance briefly at the questioner, and then immediately look for friendly individuals in the audience as you begin your response.

- **Finally, do not allow the hostile questioner an opportunity to ask a follow-up question.** When you finish your answer, make sure you are turned toward the other side of the room. Keep an eye out for individuals who look eager to raise a friendly question, and recognize one of them as soon as you conclude your answer.

How Should You Address a Silly Question?

It is almost as important to maintain your composure with a silly question as with a hostile question. Be careful not to be impolite or look impatient or bored with the question. Because some people in the audience may feel embarrassed or annoyed by a silly question, try to make the audience feel at ease by responding briefly and politely. For example, if someone asks you a question about a point you already covered thoroughly, you might say: "As I mentioned earlier, there is no simple solution to this problem. But we'll keep looking for answers." Then go on immediately to another question. As with a hostile questioner, don't allow someone who asks a silly question to follow up with another.

 WRAPPING UP Q&A

If you sense that the audience is getting restless or that you have used up your allotted time, don't cut off the Q&A session too abruptly. You can bring it to a close by looking at your watch and saying, "We have time for one more question." After that if people have more unanswered questions, you should invite them to speak with you after the presentation, when you can exchange business cards, phone numbers, or e-mail addresses. When you have answered the final question, thank the audience for their attention and take your seat. There is no need to add any concluding remarks.

Communication consultant and public speaking coach David Sandler sums up the inherent value of an extemporaneous question-and-answer session after a prepared presentation, saying that "a strong Q&A segment often turns an average presentation into something much more memorable. The segment provides a chance to embellish, clarify and enrich the earlier comments, which in turn helps the audience further absorb your information and solidify a positive impression of your speaking ability."

Sandler offers "Six Rules of Engagement" to maximize the effectiveness of Q&A, which nicely complement the strategies presented in this chapter:

Rule 1: Establish a personal connection with the person asking the question.

Be as welcoming to the person asking a question as you would to a guest visiting your home for the first time. You will accomplish this by establishing eye contact and projecting a friendly expression as you casually move closer to the individual, and extending an open palm in their direction as a way of connecting with the person.

Rule 2: Do not lose the audience while responding to the individual.

Even the best speakers forget to shift their focus from the individual to the group at times. But take care not to focus too long on "the most interesting person at the party."

Rule 3: If you cannot answer a question, do not pretend that you can.

"An effective approach for responding to a question that you cannot answer is to compliment the person on the question or point they have raised, and acknowledge that you do not have a response at that moment."

Rule 4: Recognize that questions typically mean you have succeeded in connecting with your audience.

In most instances people are asking questions because you have hopefully piqued their curiosity, so you want to be as receptive as you can in sharing information with the person.

Rule 5: Refrain from engaging in a battle of wits.

You do not want to get locked into an intellectual battle with someone in your audience, and even if you are the so-called expert, nobody owns the truth. The "agree to disagree" approach allows both parties to "win" their argument, but more importantly, allows you as the focal point, to move on to other questions, and not allow one person to dominate the discussion.

Rule 6: Be prepared to fill the sound of silence.

What if you ask for questions when you have finished your formal comments and there are none? Those few seconds can be extraordinarily awkward, leaving the impression that your speech really didn't capture the attention of your audience. . . . You will combat that eternity of silence by having your own question for the audience in your back pocket.

David Sandler summarizes the important role Q&A plays in a presentation this way:

Your prepared comments provide the narrative and overall frame for your presentation. But the Q&A section is the dialogue, the spontaneous exchanges representing a chance to re-frame your material, insert additional information, or share stories that are stimulated by a thoughtful question. Understanding that your audience's questions provide you with an excellent opportunity to make a good presentation even stronger is all part of being an accomplished public speaker.

 ## CONCLUSION

Just as Bill discovered with his speech on bio-diesel fuel, there are commonsense strategies you can use to prepare for a question-and-answer session, to establish some control over it, and to handle Q&A in such a way that it enhances your presentation and makes you look good. Remember that with Q&A you are sharing the power of the podium with your audience. Be positive about the Q&A session. It's all part of *your* presentation.

TIPS AT A GLANCE FOR HANDLING A QUESTION-AND-ANSWER SESSIONS

- Start with the right mind-set about the inherent value of question and answer (Q&A).
- Anticipate possible questions while preparing and rehearsing the presentation.
- Set guidelines for Q&A.
- Provide a segue to Q&A.
- Establish a connection with the person asking a question.
- Repeat or paraphrase questions for the audience.
- Acknowledge or compliment good questions.
- Don't lose the audience while responding to the individual.
- Prepare a response for questions you can't answer.
- Be prepared with a question for the audience if necessary.

Developing Speeches that Persuade

"Select a topic you are passionate about and include credible, relevant evidence to support your point of view."

When her instructor introduced the persuasive speech assignment, Lisa knew immediately what she wanted to speak about. She had recently seen a special report on ABC's "20/20" that drastically changed her attitudes about one of her favorite foods. Having grown up in an Italian family, some of Lisa's most memorable meals were traditional veal dishes, such as veal scaloppini and veal parmigiana. But the "20/20" report revealed what undercover investigative reporters learned about how calves are raised to produce veal, and this report shocked her and dramatically changed her attitudes about veal. After watching the program, Lisa made up her mind that she would never again purchase or eat veal. And in her speech she wants to persuade the audience to do the same.

This chapter covers the basic principles of persuasion and offers practical suggestions and guidelines for developing effective persuasive speeches. It should help you become more discriminating about persuasion aimed at you—such as the countless media "messages" we encounter each day—and also become more proficient at persuading others.

DEVELOPING AN EFFECTIVE PERSUASIVE SPEECH

In the broadest sense, all presentations are persuasive. Public speakers always want to persuade the audience that their message is important and valuable. In this chapter, however, we will discuss persuasive techniques for presentations where the speaker specifically sets out to reinforce or change beliefs or motivate people to take action. We will use Lisa's presentation to focus the discussion. Below is a transcript of her speech, "Veal: The Cruel Meal." As you read it, pay close attention to persuasive techniques Lisa uses to urge the audience not to eat veal.

Veal: The Cruel Meal

by Lisa A. Viscel
RVCC Student

1   As a kid growing up in an Italian family, there were many times when my mother or grandmother would serve veal. Some of my favorite dishes were veal scaloppini, veal Marsala, and veal parmigiana. Because veal is so expensive, these dishes were usually reserved for special occasions or holidays. As a kid, I never really thought much about where veal came from. I figured it was just another meat. That was until I watched a special on "20/20" where reporters went undercover to expose the truth about veal. What I saw horrified me! There were graphic pictures of calves, some barely a day old, chained and crated in their own waste. There were pictures of calves, dead and still chained, going unnoticed as workers walked by. I could not believe how cold, cruel, and inhumane human beings could be. Since watching that special, I have neither purchased nor eaten veal again, and after tonight I hope you will do the same.

2   According to the Animal Protection and Rescue League, farm animals, just like our pet dogs and cats at home that we love so much, feel pain and need affection, socialization, and play. Farm animals deserve the basics of life—fresh air, clean water, adequate living space, basic physical care. The veal calf receives none of these.

3   Veal calves are a by-product of the dairy industry. In order for a dairy cow to produce milk, she needs to give birth to a calf. After calving, cows will produce milk for several years, until their production drops and they are slaughtered. Fifty percent of the calves are females, which are raised to replace the old dairy cows. The other 50 percent are males. Since they cannot produce milk, they are taken from their mother immediately after birth and put in the veal crate, which is about two feet wide. The calves are usually chained in the veal crate, so they are unable to turn around or lie down. The crate prevents movement so the calves' muscles cannot develop naturally, thus keeping the meat

tender. The calves are unable to perform normal behaviors, such as grooming, and are usually left in their own waste for days at a time. The calves are fed a fatty liquid substitute for milk, purposely lacking specific nutrients and iron, so that they become anemic, making their flesh pale and sickly, just the way the producers like it. The crate has no bedding, for fear that the calf may eat it, which would make its meat a darker color, and therefore undesirable. Because the calf cannot move around, it does not burn calories, causing a lack of appetite. Farmers sometimes withhold water for days to make the calf thirsty so it will drink more of the fatty food substitute. Thirsty and lacking iron, calves lick urine-saturated slats and any metallic part of the crate to satisfy the need for what their bodies crave. The lucky calves die after a few weeks; the unlucky ones live this way for four long months until they are slaughtered.

4   According to Frank Hurnik, Professor of Animal Science at the University of Guelph in Canada, calves raised for veal require five times more medication than calves not raised for veal, just to keep them alive, making veal meat much more likely to contain harmful or illegal drug residue. Researchers have also reported that veal calves exhibit abnormal coping behaviors due to frustration, which can lead to a long list of diseases.

5   "But veal tastes so good!" you say, and that may be so. But at what price? Can we human beings really justify this cruel and inhumane treatment of newborn calf "babies" just for an expensive meal that we occasionally eat? There are so many other tasty foods to satisfy our taste buds! Eating veal is really a question of ethics, not taste.

6   According to the American Veal Association, 750,000 calves are slaughtered for veal every year in the U.S. During their brief lives these calves never see the sun or touch the earth. They never see or taste grass. Their anemic bodies crave nutrients; their muscles ache for freedom and exercise. They cry for maternal care. In their brief lives they only experience pain, isolation, and then finally death. Farm Sanctuary reports that the U.K. and other developed countries have abolished the veal crate, as well as other cruel and inhumane confinement of farm animals. Unfortunately, the United States is lagging far behind them, but you can help put a stop to this animal torture. Do not buy or eat veal!

Sources

ABC News, "20/20." Special Report on Veal Production.
The American Veal Association. *www.vealfarm.com.*
The Animal Protection and Rescue League. *www.aprl.org.*
Farm Sanctuary: Rescue, Education, Advocacy. *www.farmsanctuary.org.*
Dr. Frank Hurnik, Professor of Animal Science at the University of Guelph.
"Expert Comments about Battery Cages." *www.freefarmanimals.org.*

FUNDAMENTAL ELEMENTS OF PERSUASION

In order to develop effective persuasive speeches, we need to become familiar with the basic elements of persuasion. Mass media today continually bombards us with sophisticated advertising and marketing "pitches" that try to persuade us to choose this brand of toothpaste or that presidential candidate. On the other hand, understanding and practicing persuasion is becoming an essential skill in today's academic, business, and professional world, where to be successful we must be able to promote our ideas and convince others to support them.

The ancient Greeks, who believed that an educated person should be a proficient orator, identified the basic elements of persuasive speaking many centuries ago. Aristotle, the famous Athenian philosopher, outlined the major elements of persuasion in *Rhetoric* in 350 B.C., and they still apply today. Aristotle's three means of persuasion are *ethos, logos,* and *pathos.*

> *Ethos* refers to the audience's perception of the character, credibility, authority, competence, and goodwill of the speaker.
>
> *Logos* refers to logical and rational appeals or arguments the speaker employs, aimed at the listener's mind.
>
> *Pathos* refers to emotional appeals or arguments that the speaker employs, aimed at the listener's heart.

Aristotle and most modern authors argue that *ethos* is the most important of these qualities for two reasons. First, unless a speaker is able to establish credibility and competence, even the most convincing arguments, rational or emotional, will have little influence over the audience. Second, audiences are far more likely to accept the speaker's message if they perceive him or her as someone with character, enthusiasm, expertise, and their best interests at heart. This is why corporations and organizations are so careful to select a credible spokesperson for their products and messages. Since they know that we are more likely to respond to someone we recognize and admire, they often choose movie stars, athletes, or other celebrities to represent their products.

But a speaker does not have to be a celebrity to establish *ethos* for a presentation. For example, how does Lisa establish her credibility, authority, and competence on the subject of boycotting veal? How does she demonstrate goodwill and concern for the audience as she tries to persuade them to forgo foods they may greatly enjoy?

Lisa obviously draws heavily on personal experience for this speech, especially in the introduction. She grew up loving veal dishes and associating them with special family occasions and celebrations. So it cannot be easy for someone with Lisa's Italian heritage to give up veal. Lisa brings *ethos* to this speech by conveying to the audience how dramatically her own attitudes about veal changed, which, after all, is her motivation for giving this speech. Look at the section of Lisa's introduction where she uses first-person comments to dramatize this turn-about in her attitudes:

> *As a kid, I never really thought much about where veal came from. I figured it was just another meat. That was until I watched a special on "20/20" where reporters went undercover to expose the truth about veal. What I saw horrified me!*

Because Lisa is not a recognized expert on this topic, what can she do to establish her competence for this speech? You do not have to wave diplomas or certificates of achievement at the audience to establish competence, nor do you have to demonstrate exhaustive knowledge of your topic. But it is important to demonstrate with well-chosen facts and examples that you have adequately researched the topic and that you are well-informed and passionate about it. Early in her speech Lisa mentions two sources that show she has researched this topic: the special "20/20" report mentioned in the introduction and the reference to the Animal Protection and Rescue League at the beginning of the second paragraph. Later in the speech, she introduces three other sources, including the American Veal Association and comments from a professor of animal science, showing that she has researched the topic to achieve competence.

PLANNING AND ORGANIZING A PERSUASIVE SPEECH

Define the Proposition

Persuasive speeches have three basic purposes. They can:

- reinforce beliefs or attitudes
- change beliefs or attitudes
- motivate action

When preparing a persuasive speech, it is important to define exactly what your purpose is from the outset. The purpose statement for a persuasive speech is called the *proposition*, because it is what you *propose* for the audience to think or do by the end of the speech. The proposition is the foundation of a persuasive presentation, and you need to keep it in mind as you prepare your speech and communicate it clearly when you deliver it. Everything included in a persuasive speech should in some way explain, illustrate, reinforce, or argue for the proposition. You have a better chance for an organized, focused persuasive presentation if you can state the proposition in one simple declarative sentence. Here are three examples of propositions for specific audiences:

> For an orientation of new college students: "I want *to reinforce the belief* that effective time management is an essential college survival skill."
>
> For an oral presentation in a nutrition class: "I want *to change the belief* that whole milk is a healthy food."
>
> For a meeting of the Environmental Action Club: "I want *to motivate* you to volunteer for the annual Earth Day campus clean up."

In these examples, notice that each proposition limits itself to one specific persuasive purpose. But a proposition can sometimes involve more than one purpose. For instance, the first proposition implies that the speaker will also want to motivate students to manage their time well. In this case, the speaker should state both purposes in the proposition, but still in a simple declarative sentence:

> *"I want* to reinforce the belief *that effective time management is an essential college survival skill and* to motivate *you to use a daily planner."*

In her persuasive speech Lisa is trying to change conventional beliefs and attitudes about veal, since most people are probably unaware of how veal calves are raised, and also to motivate the audience not to buy or eat veal. Lisa's proposition appears in the last sentence of her introduction:

> *Since watching that special, I have neither purchased nor eaten veal again, and after tonight I hope you will do the same.*

Lisa reiterates her proposition in a *call to action* at the end of her speech: "Do not buy or eat veal!"

Notice that the proposition for each of the three examples mentioned above addresses concerns and needs for a specific audience—a student orientation, a nutrition class, the Environmental Action Club. When preparing a persuasive speech it is important to find out about the attitudes and values of your audience so your proposition will be reasonable and attainable for them. Lisa is assuming that most of her audience does not know how veal is raised. That is why she includes basic information in paragraph 3 about how "veal calves are a by-product of the dairy industry." But what can Lisa do to ensure her assessment of the audience is accurate and that they will accept her proposition and take the action she is urging?

Analyze the Audience

The proposition for your persuasive speech may depend on whether the audience is likely to be in favor of, opposed to, or neutral toward your message. If you can identify the audience's needs, values, and beliefs beforehand, you will be better able to define a proposition that is suited for them and to present more convincing arguments to support it. Lisa's proposition to boycott veal, for instance, would hardly have the same impact on a group of vegans. Sometimes a simple question included in the presentation can help a speaker gauge the audience's awareness of or attitudes about a topic. For example, just before the background information about veal calves in paragraph 3 Lisa might ask, "How many of you know how veal calves are selected?" Based on a quick show of hands in response to this question, Lisa would have a better sense of what her audience already knows about veal production. (Review the section "Analyzing Your Audience" in Chapter 2, as well as the audience analysis resources at the end of that chapter.)

Organize the Speech

Most persuasive speeches fall under two basic organizational patterns: *cause-and-effect* speeches and *problem/solution* speeches. In the former the speaker argues that one event or condition directly produces a specific effect, generally undesirable. In the latter the speaker identifies a problem and then persuades the audience to accept specific solutions to it. The problem/solution organizational pattern is generally more useful for persuasive speeches because it can apply to so many situations and topics. Lisa's presentation, for example, is a problem/solution speech: The problem is that the treatment of veal calves is cruel and inhumane; the solution is not to buy or eat veal. In analyzing Lisa's speech, we will examine persuasive techniques she employs to make the problem/solution format work effectively.

APPLYING LOGICAL PERSUASIVE TECHINQUES

As the root of the word suggests, *logical* appeal is where Aristotle's *logos* figures in persuasion. Logical appeal refers to the speaker's use of reasoning and argumentation to persuade the audience. Logical reasoning follows specific, long-established rules and principles, the most important of which are syllogistic reasoning, deductive and inductive reasoning, cause-and-effect reasoning, and reasoning by analogy.

Syllogistic Reasoning

A syllogism is an argument or way of reasoning in which two statements, called *premises,* support an inevitable, logical *conclusion.* For example:

> All employees of Prima Health Labs are required to wear safety goggles on the job. (*Major premise*)
>
> Gina is an employee of Prima Health Labs. (*Minor premise*)
>
> Therefore, Gina must wear safety goggles on the job. (*Conclusion*)

The point of a syllogism is that if the two premises are true, then the conclusion must also be true. The speaker's primary concern when using syllogistic reasoning is to convince the audience to accept the premises. To do this, of course, you must avoid flaws in wording the premises so that they cannot be proved untrue. Wording is especially critical with all-inclusive or all-exclusive language—words like "all" and "none," "always" and "never"—where any exception will create a "fallacy" in the premise. It is important to use such words carefully in persuasive speeches because broad generalizations will undermine your argument if the audience finds flaws in them. Let's say, for example, that Gina is a *secretary* at Prima Health Labs and is *not* required to wear safety goggles on the job. In this case the major premise is false, and so is the conclusion. More specific language is needed here to create a syllogism that is true. For example:

> All *lab technicians* at Prima Health Labs are required to wear safety goggles on the job. (*Major premise*)
>
> Jeremy is a *lab technician* at Prima Health Labs. (*Minor premise*)
>
> Therefore, Jeremy must wear safety goggles on the job. (*Conclusion*)

In actual speeches syllogisms are not presented as in these examples. However, if you pay attention, you will often notice syllogistic reasoning embedded within statements in a persuasive presentation. For example, consider the syllogism implicit in paragraph 4 of Lisa's speech, where she says: ". . . calves raised for veal require five times more medication than calves not raised for veal, just to keep them alive, making veal meat much more likely to contain harmful or illegal drug residue." In this instance the second premise is unstated: Medications produce harmful or illegal drug residues in veal calves.

Deductive and Inductive Reasoning

Deduction is a form of syllogistic reasoning from the general to the specific. If a general statement is true, then specific instances covered by the generalization must also be true. For example:

> Medical experts agree that fair-skinned individuals are highly susceptible to skin damage, including skin cancer, from prolonged exposure to the sun. (*General statement*)
>
> Colleen has fair skin. (*Specific instance*)

The logical conclusion is that Colleen, a fair-skinned individual, risks skin damage, and perhaps cancer, from prolonged exposure to the sun. The same conclusion applies to other fair-skinned individuals as well. For a persuasive speech on this topic the speaker's main concern would be to convince the audience that the generalization is true.

An example of how Lisa employs deductive reasoning appears in the last paragraph of her presentation, where she states that "other developed countries have abolished the veal crate, as well as other cruel and inhumane forms of confinement of farm animals." Then she adds that "the United States is lagging far behind," from which we can deduce that, for the United States to be considered a *developed* country, it too should abolish the veal crate.

Induction is the reverse process, reasoning from the specific to the general. For example:

> Mary, Doug, and Cynthia, all of whom have fair skin, spend the day on the beach without using sunscreen, and they all get serious sunburns. (*Specific instances*)
>
> Individuals with fair skin risk bad sunburn if they do not limit their exposure and/or use strong sunscreen. (*General statement*)

Lisa uses inductive reasoning in paragraph 3 of her speech when she cites specific inhumane treatments that veal calves suffer, which lead to the generalization in the final paragraph that "their brief lives only experience pain, isolation, and then finally death."

Cause-and-Effect Reasoning

Cause-and-effect reasoning argues that a particular situation, action, or condition produces an inevitable result. This type of argument is a highly effective persuasive technique, but it is also one of the most difficult to prove. Many medical and scientific debates, for instance, hinge precisely on whether cause and effect can be demonstrated. As a responsible, ethical speaker you must be careful not to overstate cause-and-effect assertions and be prepared to support them with convincing evidence. Here is an example of a problematic cause-and-effect assertion:

> *Prolonged exposure to the sun causes skin cancer.*

Although commonly accepted as true, this statement raises questions that might make it logically unacceptable for thoughtful listeners. Is skin cancer the *inevitable* result of prolonged exposure to the sun? Does the statement apply to *all* individuals in *every* case of prolonged exposure? How long is *prolonged* exposure? To be convincing, a cause-and-effect argument, like the hypothesis for a scientific experiment, must be based on assertions that are precisely defined and that can be defended with solid evidence. Remember, the more you ask the audience to change beliefs or to take action, the more persuasive your arguments and evidence must be.

Reasoning by Analogy

This type of reasoning uses comparison to help the audience see logical connections between a familiar concept or argument and a less familiar one. An analogy reveals similarities between two entities that are otherwise dissimilar. Here is an example of how a speaker might use an analogy in a proposition for a speech on sun protection:

> *We would be a great deal healthier if we thought of our bodies as a bottle of fine wine. We prefer them to age slowly and naturally, to*

> *maintain their finest qualities for as long as possible, and to avoid*
> *damage from harsh conditions. So it makes good sense to protect our*
> *bodies with sunscreen from harsh exposure to the sun.*

Besides providing logical support for an argument or proposition, analogy can be an effective rhetorical device to arouse interest, especially in the introduction, and to add color or humor to a presentation. An interesting analogy can sometimes provide the central metaphor or theme for an entire speech. Lisa uses an analogy in the second paragraph of her speech, where she compares farm animals with family pets: ". . . farm animals, *just like our pet dogs and cats at home that we love so much,* feel pain and need affection, socialization, and play."

 # EVALUATING AND PRESENTING EVIDENCE

To maintain credibility a speaker is obliged to substantiate assertions and defend arguments with evidence that is credible, relevant, current, and sufficient. Therefore, it is important to understand how to evaluate the quality of evidence in a persuasive presentation.

Facts, Inferences, and Opinions

Consider this hypothetical situation: Your Aunt Fran, a receptionist in a doctor's office, tells you that anorexia and bulimia are definitely on the rise across the country because their office is seeing more and more patients with eating disorders. How accurate and reliable is Aunt Fran's assertion? To answer this question we need to look more closely at the evidence that supports the assertion, the source of the evidence, and the context in which it is applied. If Fran can document, for example, that "more and more patients" means that doctors in their practice treated 15 percent more patients with eating disorders this year than last year, we can accept this data as accurate, assuming Fran is a truthful and responsible source. We might also *infer* that there *may be* an increase in cases of eating disorders across the country, if we know that Fran's office is typical of other medical practices nationwide. But based on this evidence, can we accept as fact that eating disorders are "definitely on the rise across the country"? The answer is no, because the data about the increased cases of eating disorders apply only to one doctor's office, and are applied too broadly to be reliable as evidence of a nationwide increase. Fran's assertion might be acceptable as an *informed opinion,* and might be cited as *anecdotal evidence.* But to assert as a fact that eating disorders are on the rise across the country, you need more data and supporting evidence from larger studies or surveys of eating disorders.

With persuasive speeches it is especially important, both for speakers and listeners, to distinguish clearly among facts, inferences, and opinions. A *fact* is information that can be verified or documented by independent measurements or observations. An *inference* is a logical deduction or projection based on facts. And an *opinion* is a personal belief or conclusion that may or may not be substantiated with data or evidence. Opinions, no matter how confidently held, sometimes have no factual basis whatsoever. Here is a brief example that may help you distinguish among facts, inferences, and opinions.

Damien is 7 feet tall. (*Fact*)

Damien may be a good basketball player. (*Inference*)

Damien is a freak. (*Opinion*)

Facts, inferences, and opinions may all play an important role in persuasion, so long as the speaker introduces them appropriately and does not misrepresent the kind of supporting "evidence" they provide. Here are examples of facts, inferences, and opinions Lisa employs in her presentation:

> *"According to the American Veal Association, 750,000 calves are slaughtered for veal every year in the U.S." (Fact, in paragraph 6)*

> *"Calves raised for veal require five times more medication than calves not raised for veal . . .* making veal the meat most likely to contain unhealthy or illegal drug residue.*" (Inference, in paragraph 3) [The statement* infers *that eating veal may also be unhealthy.]*

> *"Eating veal is really a question of ethics, not taste." (Opinion, in paragraph 5)*

Evaluating Evidence

There are four important questions we need to ask about evidence used in persuasion: Is it credible, relevant, current, and sufficient?

In the argument about eating disorders mentioned earlier, Aunt Fran's information is *credible* if it is limited to patients with eating disorders in that particular doctor's office. And it may be credible as informed opinion, though not as hard evidence, that eating disorders are "on the rise across the country" because it does not provide sufficient factual data to support such a claim. Since Lisa herself is not an expert on veal production, evidence that she presents will be credible if the audience accepts her sources as credible. Lisa has cited as references recognizable and reliable sources of information—a report on an award-winning television news magazine, a professor of animal science, two organizations concerned with the treatment of animals (Farm Sanctuary and the Animal Protection and Rescue League), and the American Veal Association. However, the audience should consider potential biases about veal production that these sources may reflect when evaluating Lisa's evidence. For example, what bias might we expect from the Animal Protection and Rescue League? To her credit, Lisa also cites the American Veal Association, a source we would expect to have an opposite bias. (For more about credibility of information for speeches see "Evaluating Sources" in Chapter 2.)

To say that evidence is *relevant* means that it is not only relevant to your topic but also to your audience. This is another reason to assess the audience's attitudes about your topic.

A good question to ask is: "Of all the evidence available, what is most likely to convince this specific audience to accept my proposition?" You should also check that evidence for your speech is *current,* particularly for topics about recent events, business, health, science, technology, or other fields where frequent new developments and breakthroughs may make even recent information outdated and irrelevant.

Lastly, you should determine if there is *sufficient* evidence to convince your audience. Gear your evidence to those in the audience who may be most skeptical of your proposition and most likely to challenge your arguments. If you have sufficient evidence to convince them, the rest of the audience will be convinced as well. However, try to avoid overkill. You may lose an audience with too much information and data, particularly if it includes too many statistics.

Consider the evidence that Lisa presents to support her proposition in "Veal: The Cruel Meal." What do you think are the most convincing and persuasive arguments in the presentation? If this were your speech, where might you try to incorporate additional evidence?

Citing Sources

Any presentation, written or oral, must cite credit for sources of information that are quoted, paraphrased, or summarized in it. Not to do so is plagiarism. Citing sources for an oral presentation, however, is not exactly the same as for an English or history paper. It is common practice in formal presentations to include a PowerPoint slide at the end citing references, and your speech instructor may require you to do so for important class presentations. But it is also important that you identify sources for the audience *during* the presentation, especially in a persuasive presentation where information and evidence largely determine the speaker's credibility. On the other hand, you do not want to overwhelm the audience with overly detailed source citations that may lose their interest. So, you need to compress source references during the speech. The following are some suggestions for how to do that.

First, it is critical that the audience *hear* you identify sources of information in your speech. At the beginning of paragraph 6 Lisa cites a source simply and straightforwardly when she states: "*According to the American Veal Association,* 750,000 calves are slaughtered for veal every year in the U.S." By mentioning the source, Lisa is letting the audience know that she did not pull this number out of a hat; it comes from a reliable source. Basically, the audience needs to know three things about outside information you present in your speech:

- Who said it?
- Where does it come from?
- How do we know it's reliable?

Without going overboard with details, try to cover these bases when you cite references during a speech. Sometimes just mentioning the source is enough. For example, when Lisa refers to "20/20" or the "Animal Protection and Rescue League," the audience can quickly register that these are familiar or recognizable sources and that information from them is probably reliable. In paragraph 4, on the other hand, Lisa cites Frank Hurnik as a source, a name people are not likely to recognize, so she adds that he is "Professor of Animal Science at the University of Guelph" to establish his credentials.

Meeting the Opposition

One big challenge for persuasive speakers is to recognize and address opposing viewpoints in a presentation. We call this *meeting the opposition.* In her presentation about veal production Lisa meets the opposition at the beginning of the fifth paragraph, when she says: "'But it tastes so good!' you say, and that may be so."

Why does Lisa introduce this comment, which seems to undermine her proposition? If the purpose of her speech is to convince people not to eat veal, why would she remind them how good veal tastes? By acknowledging, rather than ignoring, an obvious argument against her case Lisa is demonstrating intellectual honesty and a willingness to consider another side of this issue. And she is, in fact, using this point of opposition to strengthen her argument because she counters it immediately by asking, "But at what price?" Lisa is leading the audience toward her main argument in this speech, that eating veal "is really a question of ethics, not taste."

If you know that most people in your audience already agree with your proposition, or that they are neutral about it, meeting the opposition may not be crucial to the success of your persuasive speech. But if your audience is somewhat resistant or even hostile to your message, addressing opposing viewpoints may determine whether your proposition succeeds. Try to anticipate arguments that may be raised against your position and meet them squarely, as Lisa does. Use points of opposition to reinforce your position or to show that they do not invalidate your position. Meeting the opposition does not have to be an extensive debate. Sometimes just one point of opposition, stated simply and directly as Lisa does, can achieve the desired effect. Acknowledging at least one opposing point of view enhances your credibility and helps you focus counterarguments more effectively.

APPLYING EMOTIONAL AND PSYCHOLOGICAL PERSUASIVE TECHNIQUES

Finally, we return to Aristotle's third element of persuasion, *pathos.* There is certainly more to an effective persuasive speech than logical argumentation and convincing evidence. Aristotle recognized that great persuasive speakers also know how to arouse strong feelings and use them to influence people's beliefs and actions.

Emotional Appeal

Lisa's descriptions of the terrible conditions that veal calves undergo, especially in paragraph 3, are highly evocative. She uses graphic details "to put the audience in the picture" about veal production, particularly about the horrors of the veal crate. These details are meant to arouse emotions of disgust for veal farmers and sympathy for veal calves. The description becomes particularly unsettling near the end of the paragraph where Lisa relates how farmers withhold water and nutrients from calves to the extent that they "lick urine-saturated slats and any metal part of the crate" to satisfy their cravings. She drives home the emotional appeal in this paragraph with an ironic, dramatic summarization of the fate of veal calves: "The lucky calves die after a few weeks; the unlucky ones live this way for four long months until they are slaughtered."

There is also considerable emotional appeal in the conclusion and call to action of Lisa's speech. She reminds the audience about the horrible fate of veal calves, tying together details and images mentioned earlier in the speech but without actually repeating them:

> *They never see or taste grass. Their anemic bodies crave nutrients;*
> *their muscles ache for freedom and exercise. They cry for maternal*
> *care. In their brief lives they only experience pain, isolation, and then*
> *finally death.*

At the end of the speech, Lisa addresses the audience directly with an emotional appeal "to help put a stop to this animal torture." Her call to action is simple, direct, and forceful: "Do not buy or eat veal!"

Psychological Appeal

Even though psychological persuasion is sometimes considered unfair or manipulative, there is certainly a place for psychological appeal in legitimate persuasive presentations, especially if it complements logical arguments and evidence. Psychological appeal frequently draws upon people's unconscious needs or fears, as, for example, in television commercials about dandruff shampoos, body deodorants, or mouth washes. Lisa uses a rhetorical question in paragraph 5 to induce feelings of shame and guilt for the way we attempt to justify the cruel treatment of veal calves:

> *Can we human beings really justify this cruel and inhumane treatment*
> *of newborn calf "babies" just for an occasional expensive meal?*

Notice in particular Lisa's choice of words that reinforce the psychological impact on the audience: the first-person pronoun "we" to involve the audience in the shameful behavior; the juxtaposition of "*human* beings" and "*inhumane* treatment" to stress the contrast between these two phrases; and, most important, the use of the emotionally loaded phrase "newborn calf 'babies'" to reinforce guilt for mistreating innocent creatures.

We should observe that Lisa juxtaposes this rhetorical question, with all its psychological impact, against the point opposition that veal tastes so good. It is a formidable persuasive technique for Lisa to use psychological appeal here to shoot down this opposing argument quickly and emphatically, and to return to the main focus of her speech, that eating veal is a question of ethics, not taste.

Personal Appeal

One other persuasive technique that may figure significantly in a persuasive speech is personal appeal, when the speaker employs personal observations or experiences to exhort the audience to follow a course of action. Personal appeal is obviously tied in closely with the speaker's *ethos,* since the more credibility or authority a person has to speak on a subject the more convincing personal appeal is likely to be. Almost any persuasive speech is more effective when the speaker infuses personal experience and passion for the topic.

Lisa uses personal appeal extensively in the introduction of her speech, where she basically describes a "conversion" experience that dramatically altered her beliefs about veal. In graphic detail she re-creates her experience watching the "20/20" report and states frankly: "What I saw horrified me!" Such dramatic personal experience can bring enormous energy and passion to a presentation because the speaker, with newfound missionary zeal, now hopes to convert the audience. Lisa's personal appeal culminates in the dynamic statement of her proposition in the last sentence of the introduction: "Since watching that special, I have neither purchased nor eaten veal again, and after tonight I hope you will do the same." Lisa's use of personal experience in the introduction lays the groundwork for the logical and emotional persuasive techniques employed in the body of the speech. Lisa's personal appeal ultimately drives her message: "Do not buy or eat veal!"

 # CONCLUSION

At the end of the chapter is the transcript of another student persuasive speech, the purpose of which is to persuade the audience to support or volunteer for an organization or cause that benefits the community. In this instance the organization is the Special Olympics. This is a solid persuasive speech, but one that could be improved or enhanced with closer attention to the principles and guidelines for effective persuasion discussed in this chapter. Picture yourself in the audience listening to this presentation as you read through it. Afterward, take time to think carefully about the questions on the evaluation worksheet. If you were coaching this speaker, how could you help her fine-tune her presentation to make it even more persuasive, to have even greater impact on listeners and get them involved with the Special Olympics?

After studying this chapter, you should have a solid grasp of persuasive techniques that can serve you well, both as a citizen and consumer barraged with sophisticated advertising messages, as well as a public speaker trying to persuade others to accept and act upon messages you are passionate about. You now have tools to prepare and present a persuasive speech that would make the ancient Greeks, and your Aunt Fran, proud.

Appendix B provides additional samples of student persuasive speeches, with and without commentaries. By studying and critiquing these speeches you can further hone the skills you need for effective persuasive presentations.

Tips at a Glance for Developing Speeches that Persuade

- Select a topic that you are passionate about.
- Write a proposition in a simple declarative sentence.
- Assess the audience's attitudes about your topic.
- Organize arguments to reinforce your proposition.
- Research evidence to reinforce your arguments.
- Present evidence that is credible, relevant, current, and sufficient to support your arguments.
- Cite your sources succinctly during the presentation.
- Include at least one point of opposition.
- Incorporate emotional or psychological appeal to complement logical appeal.
- Incorporate personal experience.
- Present your proposition in the introduction.
- Provide a "call to action" in the conclusion.
- Deliver your presentation with enthusiasm and passion.

Special Olympics: Creating Special Smiles

by Ali Zofcin
RVCC Student

1   Everyone knows that a smile is a pleased, kind, or amused facial expression to show cheerfulness or acceptance. A smile is a look of favor or approval. But sometimes a smile is more than a smile. So, why do you smile? Is it because it simply comes naturally, or because you've accomplished a goal, or done something amazing? For some people to smile it takes a lot, and for others very little. But the smile on the face of a child or an adult who is racing to the finish line of the Special Olympics is more than just an ordinary smile. Today I'm here to motivate you to help create these special smiles, by getting involved with Special Olympics.

2   The Special Olympics is an international organization that changes lives by promoting understanding, acceptance, and inclusion between people with and without intellectual disabilities. Michael Weideli is 1 out of 3.5 million people who are active participants in the Special Olympics. Michael is the younger brother of one of my best friends, and every time I step into their home he shows me a newspaper picture of himself on the wall. You can feel Michael's pride and happiness when he shows me this picture. His smile is contagious.

3   So why should you get involved? To support children, adults, and the Special Olympics mission, which is: "To provide year-round sports training and athletic competition in a variety of Olympic-style sports for children and adults with intellectual disabilities, giving them continuing opportunities to develop physical fitness, demonstrate courage, experience joy and participate in a sharing of gifts, skills and friendship with their families, other Special Olympics athletes, and the community."

4   One way to get involved is on March 3rd and 4th at MetLife Stadium. There is a flag football fundraiser in which you can win autographed New York Giants football merchandise. You are guaranteed three scrimmage games on the field, locker room access, and food. All proceeds collected by the team benefit Special Olympics athletes and help support their mission. In the last five years this fundraiser alone has raised over $260,000 in New Jersey for the Special Olympics, helping over 22,000 athletes who train and compete in 24 Olympic-style sports, including events in volleyball, track and field, soccer, softball, tennis, golf, floor hockey, bowling, and skating.

5   So why should you get involved? Because not only are you benefiting others, but you could be benefiting yourself. And because it's fun. It might even be a life-changing experience. Samantha Huffman, a junior at Hanover College

and a member of the national youth activation committee that is involved with the Special Olympics, says of her experience with Special Olympics: "Everyone has that one experience that changed the course of his or her life. That one action you took or decision you made, that if you wouldn't have made it, well, you wouldn't be the person that you are today." Participating in Special Olympics is Samantha's special thing. The Special Olympics organization is her family.

6   You, too, should consider volunteering for the Special Olympics to help create smiles for young athletes and possibly have a life-changing experience.

7   Now, I understand that helping with autistic or handicapped individuals can be uncomfortable and difficult. But there are so many ways to get involved. The same goes for not having enough time or money. There are plenty of opportunities to volunteer. You can volunteer as a coach. As a coach your goal is to provide sport skills and the spirit that determines a true athlete. You are a role model, and building the athletes' character, as well as your own. There are 50 annual competitions that you can get involved with. My first year participating I helped serve lunch, but you can also be a scorekeeper, timer announcer, an athlete escort, or help with set-up, registration, and award presentations. According to Dustin Smith, a Special Olympics event volunteer, being an athlete escort is the best volunteering position. You can also go through training to become a health-care volunteer. You can donate money on their website, or you can sponsor an athlete. You can also donate physical things, like prizes for the athletes. You can even run marathons. On December 4th, in fact, there is the kick-off of the Special Olympics Holiday 3-K race and fun walk. There are lots of ways you can be involved.

8   So, how do you get involved? Well, you can go online to www.sonj.org, which is the official website of the Special Olympics. It's very easy there to find out further information about the Special Olympics Organization and the different opportunities in which you can be active. To participate in events you are required to agree to a code of conduct, and certain events also require you to fill out a pre-event training application. For more information you can also email volunteer@sonj.org or call 609-896-8000.

9   In conclusion, I'd like to share with you the Special Athlete Oath, which all athletes participating in Special Olympics take. The oath is: "Let me win, but if I cannot win, let me be brave in the attempt." For me, this simple oath expresses all the joy, happiness, and hope that the Special Olympics represent. It inspired me to get involved with Special Olympics, to make a difference in some young athlete's life, to help create that special smile on Michael's face. I hope that after hearing about these opportunities you also feel motivated to get involved with Special Olympics, not only as a volunteer but also by spreading the word about the work of this wonderful organization. And if you know anyone who is

eligible to participate in Special Olympics as an athlete, I hope you will encourage them to get involved as well. So, please, get involved with Special Olympics. Help create more special smiles!

Sources

Samantha Huffman, National Youth Activation Committee member
Official New Jersey Special Olympics website, *www.sonj.org*
Dustin Smith, Special Olympics event volunteer
Michael Weideli, Special Olympics athlete

Special Olympics: Creating Special Smiles

Evaluation Worksheet

Proposition: Is the proposition clear and evident? Can you identify where the speaker introduces it? Can you restate the proposition in a simple declarative sentence?

Organization: What organizational strategies has the speaker employed to unify the presentation and help it flow smoothly? From a listener's perspective, where do you see opportunities to enhance the flow of the speech?

Speaker Credibility: How has the speaker established her credibility and competence for this presentation? Do you think she has done so adequately? Why or why not?

Logical Persuasive Techniques: What arguments does the speaker employ to persuade the audience to volunteer for Special Olympics? Do you think the logical appeal of the presentation is adequate? Why or why not?

Evidence: What evidence does the speaker introduce to reinforce her arguments? Is the evidence credible, relevant, current, and sufficient? Why or why not?

Meeting the Opposition: Where does the speaker introduce points of opposition? Do they adequately anticipate reasons that may be raised for *not* volunteering for Special Olympics? Why or why not?

Sources: Are the outside sources cited for the presentation credible, reliable, and appropriate for the presentation? Why or why not?

Emotional and Psychological Persuasive Techniques: What emotional or psychological techniques does the speaker employ to persuade the audience to volunteer for Special Olympics? Do you think they are adequate for the presentation? Why or why not?

Introduction: Does the introduction adequately arouse audience interest, establish speaker credibility, and introduce the proposition? What opportunities do you see to enhance the introduction's impact on the audience?

Conclusion: Does the conclusion adequately wrap up the speech, reinforce the speaker's interest and commitment, and leave a lasting impression? What opportunities do you see to enhance the conclusion's impact on the audience?

Preparing and Delivering Team Presentations

"No matter what its specific purpose and goals may be, a critical underlying purpose for any team presentation is to showcase the skills and expertise of the team itself."

Jeff recently completed a degree in computer science from a big-name university, and a small electronics firm hired him to head up a team of five people to select and install a new computer network for an important client. Three weeks into the project, Jeff received an e-mail from the client's marketing director, asking him to present a progress report to their senior staff. Jeff was elated. He would finally have an opportunity to showcase his presentation skills, of which he was quite proud. Knowing he was a confident, effective presenter in college, Jeff, dressed to the nines in his best business suit, felt ready and eager to impress the client.

Jeff requested updates from his team members and prepared an extensive 20-slide PowerPoint report about the project. On the day of the presentation Jeff arrived at the client's offices early to check out the meeting room and the projection equipment. Expecting a more formal presentation setting, he was surprised to be ushered into a small conference room that was set up for a panel presentation. Jeff was taken aback when the clients, attired in khakis and polo shirts, walked in and asked where the rest of his team was. They were obviously expecting a more informal team presentation, not a slick one-man show. Jeff immediately removed his suit jacket and rolled up his sleeves, and changed his game plan. He jettisoned most of the slides from his presentation, spoke "off the cuff" about the current status of the project, and assured the clients that the entire team was looking forward to presenting a full report in a few weeks.

Jeff managed to salvage some useful feedback from the meeting and to save face with the client, but he learned a painful lesson that day. Although he was a confident presenter with good public speaking skills, he had no experience with team presentations and consequently had no idea how to work *with* his team to prepare the kind of presentation the client was expecting.

This chapter provides guidelines and best practices for planning, preparing, rehearsing, and delivering an effective team presentation in an academic or business setting. It offers strategies for specialized presentation skills that are more and more in demand in the workplace today. The NACE Job Outlook 2012 report mentioned in the Introduction, for example, identifies "Ability to work in a team structure" at the top of the list of skills employers are looking for when they hire college graduates for new positions.

© Yuri Arcurs, 2012. Used under license from Shutterstock, Inc.

PLANNING A TEAM PRESENTATION

The obvious difference between an individual presentation and a team presentation is that more people are involved, and the key to an effective team presentation is to make the best use of all those involved at every stage of the presentation process. Therefore, Jeff's first mistake was not engaging his team members from the outset. Rather than request updates, Jeff should have called the team together for a planning session as soon as he received the client's email.

Below are some best practices that presentation skills coaches and consultants generally agree upon for planning an effective team presentation:

- **Assess strengths and weaknesses of team members.** In any given group individual skills and talents are bound to vary. Moreover, in a typical work group, the members are usually selected to balance and complement one another's areas of expertise. Therefore, to make best use of its assets, team members should honestly assess and acknowledge the individual strengths they bring to the table, as well as their limitations. Jeff may be an excellent presenter, but perhaps other team members would be better at researching, organizing information, analyzing data, or preparing visuals for the presentation.

- **Establish the purpose and goal of the presentation.** Team presentations may have widely different purposes and goals. In academic or business settings team presentations are usually either an informational "report," as for Jeff's team, or a persuasive "pitch" for some product, concept, or course of action. A team presentation may also incorporate both of these functions. In any case, a team presentation will depend on the same basic elements required of any informative or persuasive speech. (See guidelines and strategies for developing effective informative and persuasive presentations in Chapters 8 and 10.) Since so many decisions about a team presentation depend on articulating its purpose and goals clearly, it is essential that the team agree on them from the outset. Most importantly, team members must understand that, no matter what the articulated purpose of the presentation may be, its chief underlying purpose is to present the team itself as a cohesive, knowledgeable, capable unit.

- **Choose a strong team leader.** A "strong" leader is not necessarily a person who will take charge and dictate how the team presentation will proceed. A strong leader is the person most capable of unifying the team members, helping them apply their talents and expertise most effectively, and pulling together all the components that make a team presentation successful. In the business world the team leader is usually someone like Jeff, who has been hired or assigned to head up the team. But even in that situation, depending on the purpose and goal of the presentation, the assigned leader may acknowledge that another team member with more experience or expertise is better suited to lead the team. That's why it is so important to assess the strengths and weaknesses of team members early on and to agree on the purpose and goals of the presentation.

- **Frame the overall structure of the presentation.** This part of the planning process for a team presentation is basically a collective brainstorming or strategy session where team members generate key ideas or a "campaign" for the presentation. (See suggestions for "Selecting a Topic" in Chapter 2.) This phase of the planning process can be very creative, and team members who "think outside the box" sometimes make their most valuable contributions to the presentation in these sessions. It's also useful at this phase of planning for the team to use a whiteboard or adhesive flip chart pages to display brainstormed ideas on the wall so the team can physically sort and rearrange them.

- **Agree on individual roles and responsibilities.** Early in the planning process every team member should know what he or she is expected to work on and accomplish for the presentation, individually or in collaboration with other team members. And the first responsibility of the team leader is to make sure all the members understand their roles and responsibilities, and to facilitate collaboration needed for them to fulfill their responsibilities successfully. Requesting updates or interim reports, as Jeff did, does not promote enough communication and interaction among team members. If team members are unsure about exactly what is expected of them, they may be duplicating responsibilities unnecessarily, or even working at cross purposes.

PREPARING A TEAM PRESENTATION

Once team members understand their role and responsibilities, it's time to get to work on the presentation. Like any effective speech, a team presentation requires audience analysis, solid research, clear organization, persuasive arguments and evidence, and good visual aids. Here are some best practices to keep in mind for preparing an effective team presentation:

- **Know your audience.** Jeff's near debacle with his presentation occurred primarily because he neglected to learn what kind of "progress report" the client expected. Jeff assumed that, as team leader, it was his delegated responsibility to report *for* his team, not *with* them. Probably the most painful lesson that Jeff learned from this experience is how essential audience analysis is. As team leader Jeff should have conferred with his boss and more experienced colleagues at his firm before starting the report to learn more about the client, as well as, of course, with the client's marketing director herself. And if he were a smart leader, he would ask the best researcher on his team to find out everything possible about the client. Jeff needed to recall from his college speech class the whole purpose of audience analysis: To gather as much pertinent information as possible about the audience and determine how best to connect with them and achieve the purpose of the presentation.
- **Do your homework.** Solid research is the foundation of any effective presentation, and especially a team presentation. For information to be substantive and arguments to be persuasive they must be supported with facts and data that are current, relevant, and reliable. Sometimes the very purpose and goal of a team presentation is to pull together data from several different disciplines or perspectives. Every team member, depending on his area of expertise, would ordinarily be expected to research one or more sections of such a presentation. But no matter how many team members are responsible for research, it is important that the leader take responsibility for coordinating the research to ensure that all sections of the presentation are adequately researched and that they complement one another.
- **Check facts and figures.** Nothing undermines the credibility of a team presentation more quickly than inaccurate or outdated information, especially if it is introduced as supporting evidence for the presentation's "sales pitch." Remember that, no matter

what else your team presentation is pitching, it is also pitching itself. To reinforce the credibility of your presentation, you want the audience to be convinced that your team is competent and well-prepared. During the preparation phase it is good practice to have team members not only check the accuracy of information they provide individually for the presentation but also to fact-check one another's material. A team member who is especially "detail oriented" may the person best suited to oversee fact-checking.

- **Assemble Visual Aids.** For any team presentation, even an informal one, it is a best practice to include appropriate visual aids to help the team deliver the presentation and the audience to follow and remember it. The team should decide during the planning phase what kind of and how much A/V will be needed, and how technologically "polished" it should be to achieve the presentation's goals. In instances such as Jeff's presentation, a slick 20-slide PowerPoint show would have been overkill for a progress report, and it would have more likely alienated the clients' staff than won them over. Jeff was smart to jettison most of his slides. However, there are also situations where sophisticated high-tech visual aids may have exactly the right impact on the audience. Visual aids provide an excellent opportunity for a team to display its creativity and personality, so it might be good planning to pair up creative and tech-savvy team members to be responsible for developing them. There is one last concern with visual aids for team presentations that is sometimes overlooked, and that is to ensure that visual aids prepared by different individuals are consistent in format and style. Therefore, it is advisable for one team member to take charge of standardizing these elements of the visual aids, and perhaps editing text as well, to ensure that the language and tone of written content is consistent across the presentation.

- **Plan ahead for Q&A.** The question-and-answer session is a very critical part of a team presentation. Since even with the best preparation the team cannot know for certain what questions may be raised, Q&A can sometimes be the x-factor that makes or breaks a presentation. But a team of presenters has to be concerned not only with *what* questions the audience will ask, but also with *who* should respond to them. It is not likely that every team member will be knowledgeable about every aspect of the presentation, nor that team members will be equally adept at thinking on their feet for spontaneous interaction with the audience. Therefore, it is important for the team to start thinking about Q&A early in the planning and preparation stages and to decide how they want to take questions, whether after each presenter or at the end, and how they will respond if they don't know the answer to a question. (See Chapter 9, "Handling the Question-and-Answer Session," for more Q&A strategies.)

- **Select one team member to serve as lead presenter.** A team presentation needs one person to serve as the "lead presenter." It will be this person's responsibility to introduce the other team members as well as the presentation, to provide transitions between different sections of the presentation, and to serve as moderator for the

Q&A or discussion session afterward. Even though it may seem easier and more practical for team members to introduce themselves and provide segues for one another as the presentation moves along, it is better to designate a team member with especially strong presentation skills or an engaging personality to fill this role. Sometimes the lead presenter may actually serve as a moderator for the entire presentation—more of a master of ceremonies than a presenter. The team leader need not be the lead presenter. If another individual is better suited to lead off, the team should take advantage of that person's abilities and expertise. But it is best to select the lead presenter during the preparation phase, well before actually rehearsing, because the responsibilities of the lead presenter require special preparation as well.

REHEARSING THE PRESENTATION

As pointed out in Chapter 6, "Rehearsing a Speech," accomplished public speakers take time to rehearse their speeches because they understand from experience that careful preparation is the surest way to anticipate and correct problems with a presentation and to eliminate obstacles that interfere with effective delivery. Therefore, any team member who will be presenting should take time to rehearse her section individually and make every effort to smooth over any rough edges, either in content or delivery. In addition, the team needs to take time to rehearse together. Here are some best practices for rehearsing a team presentation:

- **Rehearse the entire presentation at least once.** It is certainly bad judgment for a team not to plan a group rehearsal at all, but a group rehearsal can be inadequate, or even counterproductive, if done haphazardly. It is important that the team rehearse and *time* the entire presentation at least once. A quick run-through to check A/V or for team members to summarize or highlight their part of the presentation is not enough rehearsal. The team needs to know confidently that each presenter's section is organized and focused to meet its allotted time limit and that the overall presentation will also fall within its allotted timeframe. If the presentation is one of many at a conference or convention with a tightly scheduled program, for example, there is no allowance for a presentation to run overtime. It goes without saying that each team member must come fully prepared for the group rehearsal and that complete visual aids should be assembled and checked beforehand. The team rehearsal is not the time to try out new ideas or strategies for the presentation that should have been decided in the planning and preparation stages. After the rehearsal team members should objectively critique one another and the overall effectiveness of the presentation. Ideally, the team should make appropriate adjustments on the spot and do a second timed run-through.

- **Rehearse with a small audience and invite feedback.** It is important for team members to provide one another feedback, of course, but sometimes team members who are immersed in the project do not have enough distance to evaluate its effectiveness objectively. We know that people who are too closely associated with a topic "sometimes can't see the forest for the trees." That's why another best practice for rehearsing a team presentation is to invite a small audience to listen to the presentation and offer feedback. It's the same reason that big theater productions take their show on the road for preview performances before their big opening on Broadway—to work out kinks in the show and find out how people will react to it. Your preview audience may be colleagues or friends who have expertise relevant to your presentation, in which case they can offer comments about both the content and the delivery of the presentation. But even if the preview audience does not have that expertise, they may be able to offer insightful observations from the perspective of a "general" audience. If there are sections of the presentation that aren't entirely clear or that haven't quite gelled yet, ask listeners beforehand to pay particular attention to them. After the presentation invite feedback. Urge your listeners to offer comments that are substantive and specific; ask them not to be hesitant to point out weaknesses in the presentation. Be sure to thank them afterward for helping your team prepare for its big opening performance.

- **Record the rehearsal and critique the video collectively.** Feedback from a preview audience is always useful, but if a team really wants to see how their presentation comes across, nothing is better than watching a video of it. The real value of recording the rehearsal comes from critiquing the video. If done supportively, honest constructive criticism can help each team member polish his segment of the presentation as well as his individual presentation skills and, consequently, enhance the impact that the entire presentation will have on the audience. Critiquing a rehearsal supportively can be an important team-building exercise in itself, one that will reinforce the underlying goal of any team presentation, which is to present the team itself in the best possible light. There are also good reasons, of course, for recording and critiquing the actual presentation.

- **Rehearse the introduction, transitions, and conclusion separately.** Chapter 3, "Developing Introductions and Conclusions," stresses that the introduction and conclusion of a presentation can have a powerful impact on the audience, perhaps greater than any other sections of it, because the introduction and conclusion are where the speaker has the audience's greatest attention and because they are what audiences remember most from a presentation. Chapter 3 also offers tips for how to prepare the introduction and conclusion effectively, one of which is to practice them separately. The team should consider the introduction and conclusion of the presentation as independent components of the presentation, as mini-speeches with their own essential functions, that serve as "bookends" for the presentation. They deserve individual attention. (Team members should take time to review Chapter 3 carefully for more tips about how to develop an effective introduction and conclusion.) Another crucial concern for team presentations are transitions from presenter to presenter, which should provide a smooth flow to help the team stay connected and on message and to help the audience follow these connections. Conversely, if these transitional moments are awkward or abrupt, they can disrupt the flow of the presentation or throw individual presenters off their stride. The team should prepare transitions beforehand, perhaps even script them, and rehearse them separately, along with the introduction and conclusion. Transitions are key elements of a team presentation and should not be left to chance.

- **Schedule a final review session just before the presentation.** Even if your team has prepared and rehearsed the presentation thoroughly and everyone feels raring to go, it's good practice to schedule a brief session shortly before the presentation for the team to review the game plan one last time and reassure one another that the presentation will be a success. An available classroom or conference room is the obvious location of choice for the presentation. But any room or space will suffice as a "green room," as long as everyone can focus on the task at hand without unnecessary interruptions. "Shortly before" the presentation doesn't necessarily mean *immediately* before, since that may not always be possible. What's important about this final session is that all team members are completely clear about the presentation plan so there won't be unexpected glitches to throw presenters off track.

DELIVERING THE PRESENTATION

Finally, here are some guidelines and suggestions to help the team make the most of all its careful planning and preparation, and to deliver the presentation with a bang:

- **Dress smartly and professionally.** For any occasion where others are forming opinions of you based partly on appearance, it is important to find out beforehand how they are *expecting* you to dress. This is especially true for a team presentation because the audience will be forming opinions of the presenters not only as individuals but also as representatives of the entire team. Therefore, the preparation phase for the presentation should include research about the "culture" of the audience—their values, concerns, and expectations, including expectations about dress code. The team should decide on presentation attire together based on that research. Jeff erred in assuming that his clients were expecting a formal business presentation. He over-dressed but, fortunately, was able to make an easy adjustment by removing his jacket and rolling up his sleeves. It would have been a more serious faux pas if he showed up in a casual polo shirt and his audience arrived in business attire. Therefore, it is usually better for team members to over-dress slightly for the presentation.
- **Pay attention to the audience.** In addition to getting to know your audience before a presentation, it is also important, as Chapter 2 points out, to get to know them

during the presentation. Even though team members certainly should be paying attention to the presentation as their colleagues are speaking, they should be paying attention to the audience as well, watching for nonverbal indicators, such as facial expressions and body language, which reveal their reactions. Experienced speakers who know how to use eye contact effectively notice such indicators and are able to make small adjustments while they are presenting based on their on-the-spot readings of audience reactions. A team of presenters has to be able to do the same, and to plan for it. The team leader especially has to pay attention to the audience during the presentation to help team members keep the presentation focused on the needs of the audience. Watching the audience can also help the team anticipate questions or concerns that might be raised during Q&A.

- **Stick with the game plan.** Capable presenters should be flexible enough to make minor adjustments on the fly based on their reading of audience reactions, but that does not mean they have license to adjust or change any major talking points or arguments, or to disrupt the overall structure and flow of the presentation—all of which the team should have discussed and decided in the planning stage. It is important that team members stick with the game plan and not embellish or ad lib in any way that may jeopardize the purpose and goals of the presentation or undermine the effectiveness of another presenter. For one presenter to inadvertently shift the focus or direction of a team's presentation is usually a recipe for disaster. On the other hand, Jeff was entirely right to scrap the game plan for his presentation because it was all wrong to begin with: It was never a team presentation.

- **Present as a cohesive, capable team.** As the culmination of all the above best practices for delivering a team presentation, it is necessary to reiterate that, no matter what its specific purpose and goals may be, a critical underlying purpose for any team presentation is to showcase the skills and expertise of the team itself as a cohesive, capable unit. This means, for example, that team members should avoid challenging one another or arguing during the presentation. If there are differing or minority positions to be aired, team members should discuss them beforehand and present them dispassionately and professionally for the audience's consideration. Naturally, any persuasive presentation is expected to "meet the opposition," that is, to introduce questions or differing points of view that offer counterarguments to the main proposition, but these points of opposition should be prepared beforehand and introduced to help reinforce, not undermine, the presentation's purpose and goals. The team leader is ultimately responsible for helping team members work out personal or ideological differences that may interfere with successfully showcasing the team's strengths and capabilities.

- **Invite comments and feedback.** In business and academic settings, procedures are usually already in place to solicit anonymous written feedback from the audience for team presentations. Typically, a generic feedback form is distributed for the audience to evaluate how well the presentation achieved its purpose or fulfilled the audience's expectations and, often, what might make the presentation more useful or effective. Sometimes, depending on specific requirements of the situation or the needs of the audience, feedback forms may even ask the audience to rate or grade the presentation's effectiveness. If written feedback is not automatically part of the presentation setting, the team leader should request it from the audience, perhaps even providing the team's own feedback form. In addition, the team leader should let the audience know that the team welcomes further discussion or comments in person. Audience feedback after a team presentation is very valuable information, especially for a team that may be required to make presentations regularly or to present the same material to several audiences. The team should review comments and feedback carefully to better understand the strengths and weaknesses the audience perceived in the presentation and to improve individual and team communication skills. Naturally, it is not pleasant to receive comments or ratings that are negative; nevertheless, these may provide the best motivation for a team to become more capable and effective.

 # CONCLUSION

Team presentations undoubtedly require more planning preparation than individual presentations, but they also offer more opportunities. If a team works together from the outset to assess its individuals' strengths and weaknesses, choose a strong leader, and prepare a presentation focused on the needs and expectations of the audience, it can create an opportunity for each individual on the team to shine and for the team to showcase its skills and expertise. A fringe benefit is the satisfaction of experiencing the group bonding that comes with good teamwork, which, according to the NACE Job Outlook, is the quality employers most desire in their new employees.

Unfortunately, because he did not understand the particular requirements and group dynamics necessary for a team presentation nor his role and responsibilities as team leader, Jeff missed a golden opportunity to showcase his team's expertise. Fortunately, you can learn from Jeff's mistakes and, employing the best practices outlined in this chapter for planning, preparing, rehearsing, and delivering a successful team presentation, seize the next opportunity that arises for your team to shine.

TIPS FOR PLANNING AND DELIVERING TEAM PRESENTATIONS

- Assess strengths and weaknesses of team members.
- Agree on the purpose and goals of the presentation.
- Choose a strong team leader.
- Plan the overall structure of the presentation together.
- Agree on individual roles and responsibilities.
- Research your material and your audience.
- Double-check facts and figures.
- Assemble visual aids.
- Plan ahead for Q&A.
- Select one team member to be lead presenter.
- Rehearse the entire presentation at least once.
- Record the presentation and critique the video collectively.
- Rehearse the introduction, transitions, and conclusion separately.
- Dress smartly and professionally for the presentation.
- Pay attention to the audience.
- Stick with the game plan.
- Present as a cohesive, capable team.
- Invite comments and feedback.

Taking Presentation Skills to a Higher Level

*"If you want your presentation skills to continue to develop
and flourish, seek out speaking opportunities that will
continually take them to a higher level."*

Each year we offer to coach students who are selected to speak at commencement ceremonies at Raritan Valley Community College. But recently a professor who was chosen to deliver the faculty commencement address asked for assistance. This person is a full professor who has lectured in college classes for more than twenty years, who has given presentations at academic conferences, who has even delivered a keynote address at a conference. But the thought of speaking before her colleagues and the whole college community made her extremely nervous, more nervous than she had ever felt in any speaking situation. She was worried that she might not even be able to *read* her speech effectively.

What happened to this professor is not uncommon. Even people who have a great deal of confidence and experience with public speaking can feel overwhelmed if they are invited to speak in a situation that is more formal or more important, or simply different, than what they are accustomed to. For the faculty commencement address this professor is being called upon to take her presentation skills to a higher level. Being objective, she realizes that the keynote address she delivered at a regional academic conference was a longer and more substantive presentation, and certainly more crucial to her professional career. But that makes no difference here because this commencement address *feels* far more demanding and scary.

The purpose of this chapter is to help you take your presentation skills to the next level, whatever that may be for you now or in the future. There are a few common speaking situations that make people feel especially uneasy, particularly if they do not have much public speaking experience. This chapter offers some practical tips for how to handle impromptu speeches and speeches for special occasions more confidently, and also recommends some things you can do to continue developing your public speaking skills in the future.

IMPROMPTU SPEECHES

A situation that usually strikes fear into the hearts of even experienced speakers is to hear someone call on them out of the blue to "say a few words." Being asked to speak extemporaneously is especially unsettling for inexperienced speakers. But if you are called upon for some impromptu remarks, don't panic. Here are some tips that can help you:

- **Be positive.** Start with the right mind-set. Don't look at the situation as a problem, but rather as an opportunity. Good impressions, and sometimes careers, are made by demonstrating the ability to think on your feet. People who are good at impromptu speaking have learned to focus and organize their thoughts quickly. You can do this too.

- **Be composed.** Take your time and look confident. Buy a little time to collect your thoughts and relax. Greet the audience, thank the person who introduced you, and express your delight at the opportunity to speak to the group. Don't give in to nervous urges to denigrate yourself or to say something thoughtless or embarrassing.

- **Be personal.** Personal experience is usually the easiest thing to talk about on short notice. Think of an appropriate experience to begin your remarks, or as an example to illustrate your main point.

- **Be witty.** Try to think of a clever or colorful remark to open with. Even if the situation or your topic is serious, a lighthearted opening is usually appropriate. If you cannot think of a good opener, try to come up with a zinger to use as a closing remark.

- **Be focused.** Choose two or three good points that are timely, interesting, or relevant to the audience. Stick to them. Don't let your comments meander or become too complicated.

- **Be specific.** Chose one good example or anecdote to illustrate each point you want to discuss. Try to avoid generalizations and clichés.

- **Be enthusiastic.** Deliver your remarks energetically, especially the conclusion. For an impromptu speech the audience will often respond as much to your enthusiasm as to your comments.

- **Be brief.** A "few words" should be just that. Keep your remarks brief and to the point. You are not expected to deliver a formal presentation. Say your piece, say thank you, and sit down. Don't overstay your welcome. If the audience looks like it would like more, ask if there are any questions at the end.

In some situations you may be called upon to give a short speech that, while not completely unexpected, you cannot really prepare in advance. For such spur-of-the-moment presentations you may have a little time to collect your thoughts and perhaps even to scribble down a few notes. In general, for these impromptu situations you should follow the suggestions listed above. But the following are additional tips for several common types of impromptu speeches.

SPEECHES OF INTRODUCTION

Introducing Yourself

Introducing yourself to a group at a meeting or in a class can be stressful for some people. It is not always easy to decide what to say about yourself. On the one hand, many people do not feel comfortable talking about their experiences or accomplishments in front of people they don't know. They do not want to sound like they are bragging or being too personal. On the other hand, most of us would like other people to appreciate the expertise we bring to the group, as well as special qualities that make us unique and interesting individuals. Here are a few practical suggestions for dealing with situations where you introduce yourself:

- **Consider the setting.** What is the purpose of the group? How much or how often will you interact with others in the group? What is each person expected to contribute to the group? If the setting is a two-hour, one-shot advisory committee meeting, you will introduce yourself much differently than you would in a speech class, where you will interact with the same people several times a week for a whole semester.

- **Focus on your best attributes.** Speak about those qualities in yourself that are most relevant to the group, the setting, and the topic at hand. What do you think others in the group most want to know, or need to know, about you? What special experience and expertise do you have to offer this group?

- **Start with a story.** Think of an anecdote or example that illustrates the attributes you want to present. Then show how the story illustrates your connection to the group.

- **Conclude with authority.** Don't end with "That's about it."

Introducing Someone Else

Introducing someone is not a speech to be taken lightly, and it is one that you should take time to prepare carefully if the situation allows. If you are introducing another speaker, your introductory comments can have a very significant impact—positive or negative—on that person's presentation. When introducing another speaker, think of yourself as that person's agent. Your job is to represent the speaker fairly, present his or her credentials, help set up the topic of the presentation, and create some interest.

Before you introduce another speaker, be sure to talk to her. Not only will it make her feel more welcome and appreciated, it will also make your job easier. Find out what she would like you to mention about her in the introduction. Résumés are quickly outdated these days, and the speaker may have recent accomplishments that you don't know about. Find out if the speaker has a particular angle or specialized perspective on the topic.

For a speech of introduction it's very important not to overlook basic courtesies. For example, be sure you know how to pronounce the speaker's name correctly. You should also ask how she wishes to be addressed in the introduction (for example, Dr., Prof., Ms., her first name, a nickname), because the form of address you use may set the tone of the presentation. If you know the material the speaker will cover or if you have heard the presentation before, do not make predictions about the speech or preempt important points in it without permission. You certainly do not want to look foolish if the speaker needs to correct what you said, nor do you want to diminish the speaker's best material or give away a surprise conclusion unintentionally in your introduction.

Make your introduction brief. The worst introductions are those that go on too long. Don't bore the audience with information about the speaker that they already know, or that they do not need to know. To highlight everything emphasizes nothing. A good rule of thumb for introducing another speaker: The more well-known the individual, the shorter the introduction needs to be.

Presenting or Receiving an Award

Presenting an award is similar to introducing a speaker. If you are giving an award, your job is to make sure that the presentation is dignified and that the recipient is seen in the best light possible.

If appropriate, you should explain briefly the context and history of the award, and perhaps how the recipient was selected. You might also mention previous winners. Then introduce the recipient and identify his qualities and achievements that merit the award. Be effusive, but be brief, specific, and to the point. Presentations that are too lengthy can undermine the impact of the award and perhaps make the recipient feel uncomfortable.

If you are receiving an award, and know about it in advance, prepare a brief acceptance speech. The standard procedure is to thank the individual presenting you the award and the organization or institution she represents. If appropriate, you should also thank individuals or organizations that helped you achieve the award. You may also express what the award means to you personally, or to the group you represent. Use names and specific examples. Be brief, be thankful, and be witty if possible. Unless you have been specifically invited to give an address as part of the award ceremony, conclude your remarks within two minutes.

Welcoming Speech

A welcoming speech is a short, informal address that introduces and sets the tone for a larger program or event. As the word *welcoming* suggests, this is a speech intended to greet an audience and make people feel welcome and at ease. Welcoming speeches tend to be fairly perfunctory, and traditionally they include some practical functions to get a program started. In a welcoming speech you typically need to:

- Acknowledge (and sometimes introduce) dignitaries, distinguished guests, speakers, or participants.
- Remind the audience about the purpose or goals of the event.
- Provide a brief overview of the program or the event, especially if a printed program is not available.
- Establish an appropriate tone for the program or event.
- Announce last-minute changes or corrections in the program.
- Introduce the first speaker or activity of the program.

Although they may be perfunctory, welcoming speeches need not be tedious or boring. As with any well-organized presentation, a welcoming speech should have an effective introduction to get the audience's attention and set up the message of the speech effectively. A humorous story, a dramatic example, a startling statistic, or a timely connection with a current event may all provide colorful material to open a welcoming speech or to shape it.

SPEECHES FOR SPECIAL OCCASIONS

Making a Toast

Be brief, personal, congratulatory, and upbeat. Open with a relevant anecdote or example, preferably humorous. Make one or two complimentary comments about the person(s) being honored. Conclude with sincere good wishes.

Paying Tribute

If you are invited to give a speech of tribute, your purpose will be to foster respect and admiration for the individual or group being honored, and to present the honoree in the most praiseworthy terms possible. Highlight the honoree's significant achievements, innovations, and contributions. Point out lessons that the audience can draw from these achievements and their ongoing importance to others. Sometimes it's good to choose a central theme or metaphor around which to build the tribute. But be careful to avoid clichés.

For speeches of tribute it is crucial that the speaker prepare meticulously. Every detail in a speech of tribute—from the pronunciation of the honoree's name to specific facts and dates about his or her accomplishments—takes on heightened importance since its purpose is to show respect and admiration for the honoree.

If appropriate or relevant, be personal and talk about specific positive influences the honored person has had on you or your organization. Include names and specific examples. Conclude by exhorting the audience to acknowledge the honoree's achievements with a toast or a round of applause.

Delivering a Eulogy

A eulogy is a particularly important and difficult speech of tribute because of the intense emotions that the speaker and the audience are usually feeling. A eulogy is the toughest speech some people will ever have to give. Most speakers begin by mentioning how honored they feel to speak about the deceased. They acknowledge the loss of the friend or loved one and focus on the meaning, achievements, and values of his or her life. Share those achievements with a few personal anecdotes or examples that reflect the individual's character or personality, but be especially careful to avoid clichés or examples that may be in poor taste. Don't be afraid to use a humorous example if it appropriately reflects the deceased or may be meaningful to the audience.

One word of caution: Even the most experienced speakers should expect to feel strong emotions when delivering a eulogy. Some sobbing or loss of control during a eulogy is often unavoidable. Audiences are very supportive of the speaker in such situations. If possible, allow yourself to feel these emotions during the eulogy but don't allow them to overpower you. Use pauses as needed. If your emotions become too overwhelming, be ready with a quick segue to your conclusion and end with heartfelt condolences to the family and loved ones.

 # PUBLIC SPEAKING SKILLS FOR THE FUTURE

This chapter has discussed some speaking situations that can be especially challenging. When these situations arise, remember to think of them as opportunities for growth and development, both as a speaker and as a person. Remember that if you maintain your composure and follow a few basic guidelines for dealing with these challenging situations, you will come through them successfully.

Like the seasoned college professor who felt inordinately nervous about delivering a commencement address before her colleagues, you may also feel overwhelmed at some time in your life by a speaking engagement that demands something extra of you. But like that professor, after you negotiate a demanding situation successfully, you will also feel a tremendous exhilaration and sense of accomplishment that comes with taking your presentation skills to a higher level.

As stated in the introduction of this book, public speaking is a skill for life. You may think that your public speaking career is behind you once you have finished your speech course or workshop. But you never know when you may be called upon, or feel compelled, to speak up about a subject that is vitally important to you. If you have committed yourself and invested some energy into mastering the guidelines for public speaking outlined in this handbook, be assured that you have acquired the essential skills you need to meet these speaking situations confidently.

But just for good measure, the following are three more things you can do to continue developing and refining your public speaking skills in the future.

Pay Attention to Other Speakers

Students in speech classes often comment, "After this course I can never listen to a public speaker the same way again." If this statement is true for you, it is a good indication that you are more attentive to good presentation skills than you were before. Whether it's a sermon at a religious service or a televised State of the Union Address from the President of the United States, we come into contact with countless public speakers in our lives. You can learn something from every one of them if you listen attentively and take note of the speaker's strengths and weaknesses. To say that "public speaking is a skill for life" also means you should continue listening to and critiquing speakers after the semester or the workshop ends. When you see a truly masterful speaker, observe her or him closely. Watch for the subtleties of timing and delivery, the emotional intensity, the close connection with listeners that enable the speaker to persuade or entertain the audience. Visualize yourself giving the same presentation, projecting the same dynamic, confident persona as the speaker before you. Imitate and emulate what you like in the speaker's presentation; make it your own.

You can learn from ineffective speakers as well. Watch for behaviors that betray insecurity, lack of confidence, or lack of preparation; and resolve to avoid them, or to control them, when you speak. Watch for cues that betray how an ineffective speaker loses confidence or the audience's interest, and imagine how you might handle that moment better. Knowing what you want to avoid in pubic speaking can help you focus better on what you want to project.

Recognize Your Own Strengths and Weaknesses

Do you recall the example in Chapter 4 of Miriam, who repeatedly used "you know?" as a vocalized pause when she spoke? Miriam eventually learned to control this verbal tic because her friend Tina helped her "monitor" it. Many of us have similar habits ingrained in the way we speak and present ourselves. We are not going to change or eliminate these habits overnight. But, again, if we think of public speaking as a skill for life, we have plenty of time to work on them. We need to remind ourselves that becoming a masterful public speaker is an ongoing process of reinforcing good presentation habits and eliminating bad ones.

So, decide what you want to reinforce and what you want to eliminate, and monitor these behaviors in yourself. If you concentrate often enough on slowing down your speaking pace or making better eye contact with people during informal conversations, you will have better control over these behaviors in more formal speaking situations. And you will become a more confident public speaker by continually honing your presentation skills in nonthreatening situations.

Accept Speaking Invitations

Why wait around for a public speaking opportunity to arise? There are many low-stress situations where you can hone your presentation skills, if you open up to them. Think back to some of the people you read about in this book who sought out opportunities to address audiences: Donna, for example, who joined the speaker's bureau at the public library, or Eleanor, who addressed the Rotary about creating more leisure time in their busy lives. It is true that these people accepted speaking invitations partly because they learned to enjoy public speaking. But you can also learn to enjoy public speaking, if you begin with situations that are not too intimidating. Start with something easy, like reading a story for preschool children, giving tours to visitors on your campus, or volunteering to read scripture at religious services. With the rising interest these days in service learning on college campuses and community service in the corporate sector, there are many opportunities to polish your presentation skills in low-pressure speaking situations. Eventually, you may feel confident enough to run for office in the student government election, sign up for a speaker's bureau, or teach an adult education course.

 # CONCLUSION

In the introduction of this book we offered this guarantee: If you make a commitment to public speaking and put some effort into it, you *will* become a more competent and confident public speaker. If you have read this handbook and put into practice the basic principles of public speaking it outlines, you *know* that your presentation skills have improved, perhaps dramatically. But have you taken these skills as far as they can go? Probably not. Do you want to see them continue to develop and flourish? If you do, seek out speaking opportunities that will continually take your presentation skills to the next level.

We leave you with this blessing: May the skills that you have learned about public speaking from this book open many doors for you in the classroom, in the workplace, and in your personal life. When they do open, feel free to drop us a note or an e-mail to relay your success story. Your story may lead off one of the chapters in the next edition.

A P P E N D I X   A

SAMPLE STUDENT POWERPOINT PRESENTATION

The following set of PowerPoint slides served as visual aids for a student problem/solution speech on the topic of plastic pollution in the oceans. Using the guidelines in Chapter 5 for preparing and using visual aids, review and critique the effectiveness of these visual aids. Consider their content (both literal and visual), organization, and design. Where do you see opportunities to improve or fine-tune them?

Plastic Pollution

SAVE MY OCEANS

By Dylan Adams

Problems Adding Up

What Did Wildlife Do

Where We Fit In

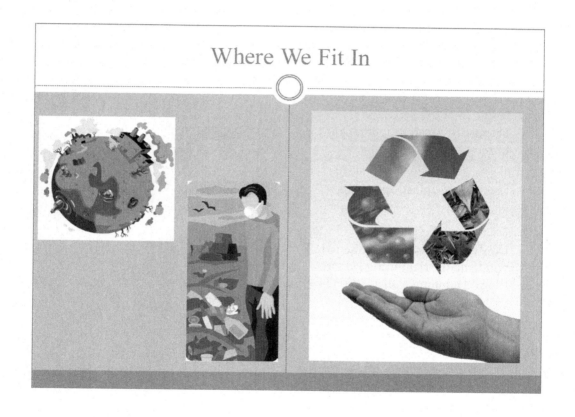

Movement for Solution

Things you can do:

- Dispose of Trash Properly Don't Litter

- Use reusable plastic products

- Don't wait for someone else to tell you to do the right thing Report Illegal Dumping Call 1(800)974-9794

- Vote responsibly

- Join Oceana
  http://oceana.org/act/donate

- Share with a friend

The End

Work Citied

- http://www.onnl.com/earth-matters/wilderness-resources/photos/the-15-most-toxic-places-to-live/china-river-indonesia

- http://oceana.org/en/eu/home

- http://www.dailybeast.com/2003/12/24/albatross-chicks-die-from-plastic-pollution-in-the-north-pacific

- http://www.dailymail.co.uk/sciencetech/article-1268559/How-killed-paradise-plastic.html

A P P E N D I X   B

SAMPLE STUDENT SPEECHES

Five sample student speeches are included for examination in this appendix. These are four- to five-minute persuasive speeches presented by students in college public speaking classes. They are basically solid speeches, but they could be even more effective and persuasive with some minor revisions. The first two speeches include comments and suggestions afterwards about how they might be improved. The last three speeches you may critique on your own.

Cut It and Leave It

Anonymous
RVCC Student

1   I know it wasn't a particularly tough winter, but I really enjoyed it when the temperature first hit 70 degrees a couple weeks ago. It was nice to be warm again. This is unusual for me; winter has always been my favorite season. Maybe I'm getting old. Then again, for me, summer always means long hours of trudging behind a lawn mower with sweat pouring down my face, into my eyes, all for results that no one really enjoyed. And, I'm not alone. Every year, many people waste both time and money on unnecessary or counterproductive lawn-care strategies. For me, though, that has changed.

2   I started thinking seriously about lawn care a couple years ago when the Township Recycling Commission (which I currently chair) was looking for ways our residents could handle their yard trimmings in a more environmentally friendly way. A startling statistic from the New Jersey Department of Environmental Protection is that, in communities where they are collected, grass clippings may account for as much as a third of summertime municipal solid waste.[1]

3   In addition to solid waste issues, there are significant problems associated with the use of weed-and-feed chemicals. The director of the South Branch Watershed Association told me that runoff from lawns treated with these chemicals is a big source of the non-point-source pollution that affects our streams and rivers.[2] There is also a potential poisoning hazard for children and pets. The ASPCA National Poison Control Center Web site recommends that pets (and presumably children) not be allowed on any area sprayed with insecticide or weed killer until the lawn is totally dry, if at all.[3]

4   For these and other reasons, we followed the lead of other communities in New Jersey and started promoting a "Cut It and Leave It" lawn-care strategy to help residents avoid the drawbacks of traditional lawn-care tactics. It's really amazing how a few simple changes in the way you cut your lawn can save you time and money, and help the environment. Even so, most people have a great resistance to trying something new, especially if they think they are messing with success. When it comes to "Cut It and Leave It," a lot of this resistance comes from a number of myths that are accepted as facts.

5   The first lawn myth is that you have to work hard to get results, that it can't be that easy. Well, yes it can. Using a "Cut It and Leave It" method is as simple as the name implies: You just leave the grass clippings where they fall when you mow. The key is that you want to be sure to let the grass grow to at least three inches high before you cut it, and then only cut the top third of the blades. Leaving the grass between 2 1/2 and 3 inches preserves the prime food-producing part of the plant. Since the grass has plenty of food-production capacity, it doesn't need to grow more, and will grow more slowly, which increases the time you can go between mowings.

6   Closely related to the hard work myth is the belief that you must play an active role in preventing weeds. But a "Cut It and Leave It" strategy will keep the lawn healthy naturally, and a healthy lawn will choke out most weeds naturally. Higher grass shades the soil, which prevents scorching, and improves the health of the grass roots. It also deprives any weeds of the sunlight they need to grow. The Web site "Organic Lawn Care for the Cheap and Lazy" humorously emphasizes this point with the dictum: "Shade is weakness, disease, and death."[4]

7   Then there is the myth that grass needs fertilizer. Well, grass does need nutrients, especially nitrogen, but most nutrients are available in average soils, and those that are not can be added judiciously, in small amounts. The fact is that most lawns that have had chemical fertilizer applied have been over-fertilized. Expensive fertilizer just creates excessive grass growth that requires endless mowing. What's worse, when coupled with overly short mowing, which traumatizes the grass, the grass ends up using all the fertilizer it gets to replace its natural food-production capacity instead of improving the strength of its roots, which allows weeds to take over, and you've just spent a lot of time and effort to grow a healthy crop of weeds. According to Spring Green, a nation-wide lawn maintenance company, up to 15 percent of the food value of fertilizer applied can be returned to the soil simply by letting grass clippings lay.[5]

8   After about two years of leaving grass clippings where they fell, I looked at my own lawn recently and thought, "Damn, it works." Even without adding any fertilizer, the brown spots are almost gone, the lawn is lusher, and there are few weeds visible. I wish somebody had told me years ago that I could get good results with less work and less expense, plus less stress on the environment. "Cut It and Leave It" is definitely a worthwhile strategy for lawn maintenance.

Sources

1. "Grass . . . Cut It and Leave It." Pamphlet, NJDEP.

2. Marie Knesser, Director, South Branch Watershed Association.

3. www.napcc.aspca.org/smalanml.html#garden. ASPCA National Poison Control Center Web site.

4. www.split.com/lawn/. "Organic Lawn Care for the Cheap and Lazy."

5. www.spring-green.com/. Spring Green, Inc. Web site.

70° Winter, person. Summer = sweating
Unnecessary/counterproductive strategies
Statistic, DEP - clippings=1/3 summer
MSW
Problems w/weed-feed chemicals
Marie: runoff = factor in non-point source
Poisoning - ASPCA National Poison Control
Center Web site
Myths: **1) Work hard for results**
      3" before cut top 1/3 of blade
      2-3" preserves food-producing part
      grows slower > time between mowings
2) Related: active role to prevent weeds
      C&L strategy healthy/ choke weeds
      Higher shades soil, protects roots
Web site "Organic Lawn Care for the Cheap
& Lazy" - "Shade is weakness, disease &
death"
3) Grass needs fertilizer---nutrients in soil
      Expensive fertilizer ⇒ excessive growth
      endless mowing
      Short mowing = traumatizes grass
      tries to regain food production
      Spring Green: ≤ 15% food value return
Personal results

Speaker's Note Card for "Cut It and Leave It"

COMMENTS AND SUGGESTIONS

- "Cut It and Leave It" is the obvious title for this presentation. But it would be even catchier and more memorable if expanded into a two-part title and incorporated into the introduction at the end of paragraph 1. How about a two-part title that ties it in with "lawn myths" introduced later in the speech?

- The speaker uses personal experience effectively in the introduction to connect with the audience. But he needs one more sentence at the end of paragraph 1 to introduce the topic solidly.

- We have included the speaker's note card for this presentation for your examination. But it would also be easy to create supportive visual aids for this speech by using "Problems" and "Myths" as headings, which would adequately cover all the important points the speaker wants to cover.

- The speaker should probably explain the technical term "non-point-source pollution" in paragraph 3.

- The speaker "meets the opposition" by mentioning the resistance to "Cut It and Leave It" in paragraph 4. This point should be developed more. It also looks like a good opportunity to reinforce his connection with the audience. Consider, for example, how he might change or elaborate on the phrase "most people" in order to refer specifically to his audience.

- To drive home the point of the dictum at the end of paragraph 6 the speaker could add a tag for emphasis: "Shade is weakness, disease, and death." For weeds!

- The conclusion is quite strong. But think of how much more dramatic it would be to make the very last words of the speech, "Cut It and Leave It!"

Pit Bull Story

Jodi Nutret
RVCC Student

1   Good afternoon. I'm sure you can all remember how at the beginning of the semester we all had to introduce ourselves in front of the class. Immediately, I became very embarrassed because I had to get up in front of the class for the first time with this huge black eye. I didn't want everyone to think that a bully beat me up; so I told everyone it was a dog bite, which was one hundred percent true, but I never told you the story behind it.

2   I was over at my friend's house partying and having a good time. It was starting to get late, so I gathered up all of my stuff. But I didn't want to leave without saying good-bye to the host of the party. I spotted him sitting at the table. He was talking with his sister, and his pit bull was sitting on his lap. I went over and tried to hug him from behind, and I don't know if I caught his dog off-guard or what, but he lunged at my face and bit me in the eye. Fortunately, as he lunged at me, he bumped my friend's hand and didn't hit me full force.

3   The next day I went to the emergency room to make sure there wasn't any major damage done. The nurse told me that my whole inner eyelid was scratched and it was a millimeter away from my cornea. This made me think. "I nearly lost my eye." Now that's really scary.

4   I had always heard that pit bulls were nasty dogs, but now that this had happened to me, I wanted to find out for myself just how true this was. I went to the library and did a little bit of research and some of the information I found was really amazing. I read an article in *The Economist* that said that pit bulls account for two percent of the dog population in the United States, but they have been responsible, since 1983, for 20 of 28 deaths caused by dog bites. This is an incredibly large number. Also in this article, I read that fifty cities in the U.S. have laws restricting the ownership of pit bulls, either by requiring the owners to take out huge insurance policies or by threatening a jail sentence if their dogs attack. In addition, this article also said that in 1987, Major Edward Koch proposed a ban on the sale or possession of pit bulls in New York City. Those who already own them may keep them, but must register them each year with the Health Department, must get them spayed or neutered, and must take out $100,000 in bite insurance.

5   An article I read in *GQ Magazine* said that in Washington, D.C., owners of pit bulls are required to muzzle their dogs when off their property and buy special liability insurance to pay for any injuries they might cause.

6   The problem with pit bulls not only exists in the United States. An article in *New Scientist* said Britain passed a Dangerous Dog Act, which made it an offense to own a pit bull that is not insured, neutered, tattooed, and implanted with an identifying chip. This act also makes it illegal to take a pit bull off your property without a muzzle or leash. Offenders can be fined $2,000 or jailed for six months.

7   Now, you may be asking yourself why there are so many laws against pit bulls. Well, first off, they are excited very easily. The article in *The Ecologist* said that there is a chemical in the brain that causes arousal, and research has shown that this chemical is very abundant in a pit bull's brain. The abundance of this chemical is what causes them to be so easily aroused.

8   Pit bulls are also found to have a high tolerance for pain. This is caused by abundant amounts of endorphins, the body's natural painkillers, in the pit bull's brain. Pit bulls are found to be very sensitive to these endorphins, and since they generate high levels of them they have no feeling for pain. In *The Ecologist* I read that pit bulls may actually be addicted to endorphins, and that they go out and look for ways to harm themselves just to get a "rush." They are endorphin "junkies." Speaking of endorphins and high tolerance for pain, I read in this same article that a pit bull attacked a little girl for fifteen minutes. The dog's owner and two other adults basically had to sit there and watch this little girl practically be bitten to death because they couldn't stop the dog. They beat the dog until it bled, and it still kept going at her. That is really scary.

9   When I was reading through the articles that I found for this presentation, I was talking out loud a lot and telling my Mom some of the things I found, and she told me about a program that she and my father had seen on television the other night. This woman owned two pit bulls. She lived in a rural area and let her dogs run loose. They never bothered anyone until one day they got into an autistic woman's house. Naturally, this woman became very frightened and started to scream. The pit bulls immediately attacked her. The more she screamed, the more they bit at her. Finally one of the neighbors heard her and called the police. The police had to shoot the dogs in order to get them to stop.

10   These dogs are out to kill. I don't see why anyone would want a pit bull around him or her. I know from my own personal experience that I would never own one because these dogs can turn on you like that. They have such a high tolerance for pain and they are aroused so easily that they will be licking your face one second and they could have a mood swing and start biting your face off, and there is absolutely nothing you can do about it. Their jaws will just lock down on you, and they will not let go until they have finished whatever they want to do to you. Perhaps if you were a drug dealer you would want a dog like this so no one will mess with you because of your dog's reputation. But for ordinary people like us, I don't really see the need to have such a vicious animal. Why would you want to put your life in danger just for an animal?

COMMENTS AND SUGGESTIONS

- Do you think the speaker has made the proposition of this persuasive speech clear enough for the audience? Where would be the best place in this speech to present her proposition?

- The speaker's passion for this topic, stemming from her scary personal experience with a pit bull, is very powerful in this speech. And she presents some convincing evidence about the dangers of pit bulls. But do you think she has adequately "met the opposition"? It would be unfortunate for this speaker to lose credibility because of appearing to be too biased. Where do you think is the best place in this speech to acknowledge the other side of this argument?

- The speaker's personal experience in the introduction obviously provides rich material for this presentation: she should try to draw on it more in the rest of the speech. For example, consider how she might reinforce the information in paragraph 7 by referring to her experience again, perhaps adding more pertinent details about what may have aroused the pit bull that attacked her. Do you see other opportunities in the speech to use her personal experience for dramatic effect?

- The example of the brutal pit bull attack from the television program mentioned in paragraph 9 is powerful and dramatic. Imagine how effective it would be if it were incorporated into the introduction to complement the speaker's personal experience.

- Think of a memorable two-part title for this speech that could be inserted at the end of paragraph 3.

- How would you suggest that the speaker improve the conclusion of this speech? If this were your presentation, what would you want the audience to go away with at the end?

Helmets and Winter Sports

Jennifer Pecoraro
RVCC Student

1   There was a night six years ago that I will never forget. My husband and I were getting ready to go to this formal affair in NYC that we were both very excited about. When the phone rang, on the other end was his sister; she was hysterical. Her two sons had gone skiing with their school and one of them had a serious accident. How serious? Serious enough that she wanted us to get to the hospital as quickly as possible. They didn't know if he was going to make it! We arrived to find our twelve-year-old nephew, who was an aspiring football player, in a coma, which he remained in for a week. After which, he spent months in rehabilitation to get movement and eventually some coordination back in his left side. You see, the accident he had that evening was a collision with a tree—head first, not even traveling that fast, according to his brother, who was an eyewitness to the accident. This was only his third time skiing; needless to say it was also his last. Most of the pain and agony his family suffered possibly could have been avoided, had he been wearing a helmet. This is something I became painfully aware of that January night six years ago. What I am going to discuss with you today will reinforce the importance of helmets for winter sports, and hopefully motivate you to wear them as you venture outside this season to enjoy the slopes.

2   I had never thought much about the importance of helmets in winter sports until this happened. I had been planning to start my daughter skiing the following year and was just beginning to consider the need for a helmet. Most parents do put helmets on their young skiers, but as they grow older and more advanced they tend not to enforce the need to wear them. This is a mistake because as the kids become more advanced they tend to take more risks, thus putting them in danger of an accident.

3   A recent article in *The Atlanta Journal* stated that millions of skiers and snowboarders should wear helmets to help protect them from the kinds of accidents that killed both Sonny Bono and Michael Kennedy. The Consumer Product Safety Commission found in a study that protective headgear can significantly reduce the number of head injuries each year and could also cut the number of deaths in half. An article in *Ski* magazine last year confirms that 17,500 people suffered head injuries from skiing and boarding and estimated that helmets would have reduced the severity of these injuries 44 percent in adults and 53 percent in kids under fifteen; also that they would have prevented eleven deaths. Another article in *Sports Medicine Online* cited a survey taken at Sugarbush Ski Resort that showed that over the last fifteen seasons 2.6 percent or 309 of the ski injuries there were potentially serious head injuries. An average of 34 skiers, mostly

male adults, die yearly of head injuries in skiing accidents, according to the same article. An article from *UPI Science News* on the Web stated that skiing and boarding are not the only winter sports that helmets should be worn for. Sledding accounted for 55,000 emergency-room visits last year, and 8,250 of those were head injuries.

4   There are several dangers in winter sports we should all be aware of. First, there are possibilities of unexpected collisions with trees, rocks, or other people, which leads into the second danger, those other people, who may be inexperienced or skiing out of control. If you are skiing, boarding, or even sledding, you are bound to come across a few of these people. I just hope they don't plow into you without a helmet and run you into a tree. The third danger is fatigue. Many of us ski past our limits. I know first-hand because last year on my last run I blew out my knee. I just thank God it was not my head. When we are tired there are more possibilities for falls or mistakes that could land you into a tree with a head injury.

5   Now, I am aware of quite a few reasons why you may not want to wear a helmet. They are not cool, or you want to wear one of those funky knit hats that show your individuality. *USA Today* agrees with you when it says that fun sells on the slopes, not safety. There is also a minor risk with helmets of neck injuries, even whiplash, according to a recent article in *Sports Medicine Online.* In *Ski* magazine they note that skiing is already an expensive sport and that an added expense is another reason people shy away from helmets. They may also give someone a false sense of security, according to a recent article in *The Los Angeles Times.*

6   However, if wearing helmets shows even the slightest decrease in head injuries, that is enough for me. My nephew happened to be one of those statistics I mentioned earlier, and I hope that none of your parents or loved ones ever get a phone call like I did six years ago to find you in a coma after a slight collision with a tree.

Sources

Cohen, Steve & Greg Tinker. "Should You Wear a Helmet?" *Ski,* September 1999.

The Consumer Products Safety Commission. Quoted in *The Atlanta Journal,* January 8, 1999.

Gordano, Jeff. Interview on October 19, 1999.

Horowitz, Bruce. "Some See a Need to 'Resell' Sport as Safe, Regulated." *USA Today,* January 7, 1998.

Lou, Michael. *Los Angeles Times,* March 23, 1999.

"Nation in Brief Study Urges Helmets for Skiers." *The Atlanta Journal,* January 8, 1999. Online from Proquest.

Potera, Carol. "Celebrity Ski Deaths Inspire Helmet Debate." *Sports Medicine Online,* March 1998. Online from Proquest.

UPI Science News. October 16, 1999.

www.drkoop.com/news/stories/october/sled_helmets.html.

Driving and Cell Phones:
A Bad Combination

Shailender Verma
RVCC Student

1   Good morning. How many times has it happened to you that you are driving in your lane and someone cuts you off, and then you realize that person is driving like he is alone on the highway? Or you are waiting at a red light and you see a car coming up behind you in the rearview mirror, which to your horror is not slowing down? It's like you do not exist for him. Last year I was driving in my lane on a highway when a car came out of nowhere and sideswiped my car. What's the common factor in these three cases? The drivers of the car at fault were all talking on a cell phone. In my case, the driver heard her phone ringing and bent down to take her phone from her bag. Today, I want to reinforce the belief that talking on the cell phone while driving is not safe and to motivate people to stop using cell phones while driving, whether they are hand-held or hands-free.

2   Talking on a cell phone, whether on a traditional phone or a hands-free device, is just asking for trouble. A study at Virginia Tech used cameras and sensors to track driver activities in a car, and they determined that incidents and accidents occurred more often when people were talking on their cell phones. To their surprise accidents occurred more often even with hands-free phones. Hands-free devices can give drivers a false sense of security. According to the National Highway Traffic Safety Administration, the act of conversation can lead to distraction and inattentive driver behavior. It can degrade driver performance and vehicle control. And according to the Insurance Institute for Highway Safety, drivers using a cell phone are four times more likely to have a crash involving a serious injury. The report also discredits the widely accepted belief that talking on your cell phone while driving isn't risky, as long as you keep both hands on the wheel.

3   Any distraction while driving in today's traffic can cause an accident. A cell phone just adds to a long list of accident-causing distractions. In fact, it is more dangerous than other distractions because we happen to do it more often. The common belief is that driving while using a hands-free device is safe, but the fact is that driving even with a hands-free device is very dangerous. A lot of people think that since their hands are on the steering wheel they can drive well, but the fact is that people often get carried away in their conversations and they make mistakes. According to "Driving and Cell Phones" on seattlepie.com, people often mentally get into tunnel-vision mode

while talking on cell phones, and their responses are slowed down, even to situations directly in front of them. Some people would argue that talking on a cell phone while driving is the same as having a conversation with a fellow passenger. But with a cell phone conversation the person on the other end cannot tell when not to distract you or when to alert you.

4   In conclusion I would like to say that talking on a cell phone while diving, whether it is hand-held or hands-free, is as dangerous as drinking and driving. So friends, don't let friends talk and drive!

Sources

"Clark Howard's Tips: Cell Phone or Hands Free . . . No Difference (Virginia Tech study)." *The Atlanta Journal-Constitution.* June 17, 2005.

"Driving and Cell Phones." seattlepi.com. November 15, 2004.
http://blog.seattlepi.nwsource.com/soundoff/archives/003805.html.

Gianulias, Koula. "Cell Phone Study: Hands-Free Cell Phones Still Dangerous (The Insurance Institute for Highway Safety). kolotv.com. July 26, 2005.
http://www.kolotv.com/news/headlines/1688952.html.

"Is Hands-Free Actually Safer?" (National Highway Traffic Safety Administration). CNNMoney.com. June 9, 2005.
http://money.cnn.com/2005/06/09/technology/personaltech/cellphones.

Science Seminars: One of RVCC's Best-kept Secrets

By John McGill
RVCC Student

1   In my first semester here at RVCC I met my favorite professor, the best one I've ever had in my life. She was my teacher for General Chemistry I, and she is just as nerdy as I am. She would stay around after class, and we would talk about all the nerdy science things that I find really interesting. At the beginning of the year she told me that I should really check out the Science Seminars, and because of that I've always known about them. It seemed like something that everyone here at RVCC would know about. But now I know that isn't so. So, I'm curious. By a show of hands, how many of you know about the RVCC's Science Seminar series? OK, so that's five or six people out of 24. That's actually more than I expected. And that's why I'm here today to talk about the Science Seminars, which I consider one of RVCC's best-kept secrets, because it's something that's so cool at our college and yet so few students actually know about them.

2   For those of you who don't know about these seminars, you're probably wondering what they are. So what are the Science Seminars here at RVCC? Let me give you a bit of background. The Science Seminars are a series of lectures started back in 1997 by a Physics professor named Daryl Walke, who has since retired. Now they are led by Prof. Paul Schuller, a Chemistry professor who organizes them. They are not long, about 80 minutes, the length of a typical class. They are held every Wednesday at 11:30 in the Physics lecture hall in the Science Center. And they are free and open to anyone.

3   The seminars are usually presented by RVCC faculty who involved in scientific research in one field or another, but they are often led by big-name science people who teach at nearby universities, or by scientists who are working at one of the pharmaceutical or technology industries in our area. For example, one of the seminars planned for next year is with a scientist who used to work for Bell Labs, which is a really famous research laboratory. She is actually being inducted into the New Jersey Inventor Hall of Fame for her work on super conductors, which are substances that have special conducting qualities when they are really cold.

4   I know most of you are not Science majors and that you don't share the same passion for science that I do. So, you're probably saying to yourself, "Why should I care?" Well, there are some reasons you might consider.

5   First of all, they are pretty interesting, even for nonscience majors. The topics are in all areas of science and technology, and even if they are sometimes pretty specialized, they are aimed at a general audience. And the presenters always make a point of showing how their topic applies directly to our daily lives.

6   Second, the Science Seminar series for a semester can actually count as a one-credit Science Honors elective, which is awesome because all you have to do is attend the seminars and write up short summary reports about them. And at the end of semester you have an opportunity to do a short 20-minute presentation on any science topic you're interested in. I want to do that next year!

7   The Science Seminar is also an opportunity to work with a professor on independent science research, if you interested in doing that. For next semester I intend to do some kind of independent research in Chemistry and then present my own science seminar. I've already been talking with my professor about it. I think I'd like the opportunity to present my own science seminar, which is kind of intimidating, although I'm sure that after this Speech class I'll be much better at it and much less nervous.

8   And the last reason that you may be interested in the Science Seminars is that they serve free snacks and coffee! You don't have to be a Science major to enjoy free coffee at 11:30.

9   So, now that you've heard about the Science Seminar series, why not check it out some Wednesday? You can go online to find out the topics and choose one that interests you. And help spread the word about them. There's no reason in the world why the Science Seminars should be one of RVCC's best-kept secrets.